# Extending Choice

**The BBC's role in the new broadcasting age**

# Contents

# Introduction

The BBC

must adapt

as it has done

in the past

The BBC is seen by many people at home and abroad as the world's leading broadcasting organisation. Over the last 70 years it has established a name for high quality broadcasting on both television and radio which has made a major contribution to British life. It has provided a national sense of shared experience, and it has played a major role in enabling the different groups within society to understand one another.

The BBC has become one of the nation's primary sources of news and information. As a broadcasting organisation, it has entertained successive generations. Its programmes have become part of our culture. It has fostered the arts, encouraging new writers, composers, artists and performers. It has helped to educate millions of people in Britain and overseas. And it has brought credit to Britain through its international World Service broadcasts.

But British broadcasting is changing. New technology, new methods of funding and new regulation are transforming the environment for broadcasters and their audiences.

At the end of 1996, in the midst of all this change, the BBC's current Royal Charter expires. Over the last eighteen months, therefore, the BBC has conducted an extensive and fundamental review of its role and services. An effective organisation cannot stand still: as the society it serves develops and as the broadcasting market expands, the BBC must adapt – as it has done in the past – to these different circumstances. This document summarises the results of our review and outlines a vision of the BBC's place in a new broadcasting age.

QUESTIONS FOR THE DEBATE

The BBC has addressed the fundamental questions which will properly be the subject of public discussion in the Charter Renewal debate:

- **Do we need publicly funded broadcasting in an expanding market?**

- **Should it be provided by the BBC?**

- **If so, what should be the BBC's public purpose, role and objectives?**

- **What kind of programmes should the BBC make and broadcast to fulfil this public purpose?**

- **How should the BBC develop its international role?**

- **Should the BBC be a single broadcasting organisation, and if so how should it shape its services to deliver programmes as effectively as possible to their audiences?**

- **How should the BBC change the way it works as an organisation to ensure that it delivers maximum value for money?**

- **How should the BBC harness new broadcasting technologies which offer the prospect of expanded and enhanced services for viewers and listeners?**

■ **How should the BBC be funded?**

■ **How should the BBC be held accountable to the licence payer and Parliament for meeting its objectives?**

In the chapters that follow, we outline our views on each of these questions. They are the BBC's initial contribution to the full public discussion that will follow.

**This document reflects the achievements and traditions of the BBC and it describes new developments already under way. But above all, this document lays out our ideas for the future – our considered thoughts about the role and services that the BBC might offer to the British public in the 1990s and beyond. It is these ideas for the future – and not just the achievements of the past – which we believe should underpin the case for the renewal of the BBC's Charter.**

# The Changing Context

1

— **more broadcasters**

— **more choice**

— **more uncertainties**

— **more risks**

Almost everything about the broadcasting world has changed since the BBC's current Charter was issued in 1981. This process of change has been at its most dramatic over the last few years, and is far from complete.

Over the next 10-15 years the British broadcasting industry will change faster and more radically than ever before. By the year 2000, the majority of households will have access to at least 20 television channels and 15 radio stations. Some television channels will offer general entertainment for large audiences, but an increasing number will be specialist channels targeted at different interest groups. Most radio stations will offer pop or popular music, but targeted at increasingly narrow groups amongst the music listening audience.

With all these services available, audiences will split their viewing and listening time between different sectors of the market, so that audience share will be much more fragmented than it is now and no single broadcaster will have a dominant position in the marketplace.

There will be increasing competition for commercial revenue to support these channels and stations. Industry revenues will be split between at least three different sources – public funding, advertising revenue and subscription fees. On current projections, the BBC is likely to have access to a third or less of the broadcasting industry's total revenue.

The BBC's future role must take close account of these dramatic changes in the broadcasting environment. Accordingly, this chapter outlines the principal factors that will determine the future of broadcasting in the U.K. – as far as we can foresee them. It serves as a platform for all of the thoughts and ideas about BBC programmes and services that follow. It focuses on three broad themes:

- ■ The increasing importance of broadcasting in a changing and dynamic society.

- ■ The transformation of the broadcasting marketplace that is already under way and which will accelerate over the next few years.

- ■ The growing base of experience from more mature overseas broadcasting markets.

INCREASING IMPORTANCE OF BROADCASTING IN THE CHANGING SOCIETY

The evidence of the influential role that broadcasting plays in British society is overwhelming. The average British person spends approximately 40 hours per week either watching television or listening to the radio – that is nearly 6 hours a day, around one third of the average person's waking hours, and more than two thirds of the average working person's leisure hours. The U.K. has the highest level of television viewing and radio listening in Europe. Only in the U.S. do people consume more broadcasting.

The British public spends more than £6 billion per annum on broadcasting related equipment and services – of which the licence fee is less than a third. £6 billion represents £275 per household per annum, and that figure is expected to increase to over £400 at 1992 prices by the end of the decade.

**International comparison of broadcasting consumption**

| | |
|---|---|
| U.K. | 40 |
| West Germany | 37 |
| France | 37 |
| Netherlands | 35 |
| Spain | 35 |
| Italy | 33 |
| Switzerland | 32 |
| Austria | 30 |

Hours per person per week - television and radio

Source: GEAR Euro-Factbook, 1991

Perhaps most significantly of all, the British people attach considerable importance to broadcasting as a critical contributor to the way in which they think and live their lives. Successive research surveys have shown that television and radio are by some way the most trusted sources of news and information in British society; that they are the most valued and appreciated providers of entertainment and culture; and that they play a valued role in the education – both formal and informal – of people of all ages.

Broadcasting is therefore at the heart of British society. The structure and composition of the broadcasting industry, the purpose and motivation of broadcasters, and the programmes and services that they offer are vital factors in reflecting and shaping that society. But this is a difficult task for broadcasters to perform when the forces at work are as diverse as they are in the U.K. of the 1990s – for instance:

■ **The fragmentation of society into discrete social, economic, racial and religious groups; and the complex network of interlocking relationships between these groups.**

■ **Fundamental changes in the demographics of British society, particularly the progressive ageing of the population and the increasing proportion of people who are retired or semi-retired.**

■ **The changing role of women in society, with more women in full time or part time work.**

■ **The growing impact and influence of regional and local diversity within the U.K.**

■ **The U.K.'s involvement with and identity within the European Community – and the degree to which British people have travelled abroad, learnt foreign languages, and developed an interest in other countries and cultures.**

■ **The greater emphasis in British society on education, training and personal development.**

■ **The stronger demand for all public service organisations to offer the highest standards of customer care, efficiency and value for money.**

Each of these forces represents a new and complex set of challenges for broadcasters. The broadcasting industry that emerges from this period of change must be better equipped to meet them.

**A new and complex set of challenges for broadcasters**

TRANSFORMATION OF THE BROADCASTING MARKETPLACE

When the current Charter was issued in 1981, there were few broadcasting alternatives to the BBC. ITV was the only alternative on television, and there were ILR stations only in major population centres as alternatives on radio. In these circumstances, the BBC's remit was clear – to meet as many of the viewing and listening needs of the British public as possible, without being constrained by commercial objectives.

Since 1981, however, the broadcasting marketplace in the U.K. has been transformed. New technology has turned the video cassette recorder into a mass market product which is now used in more than 70 per cent of homes; enabled the

**All these changes have altered forever the balance of supply and demand in the broadcasting industry**

successful introduction of direct to home broadcasting by the Astra satellite; and supported the more hesitant introduction of cable television into the U.K.

Regulatory changes have led to the introduction of Channel 4 and soon of Channel 5; radically altered the licensing arrangements for ITV franchises; created a more relaxed regulatory regime for commercial broadcasting in the U.K.; and allowed the licensing of local, and more recently national, commercial radio stations.

All these changes have altered forever the balance of supply and demand in the broadcasting industry. There are now many more broadcasters seeking to serve roughly the same number of viewers and listeners with an increasing array of television and radio services, using several different means of distribution. This process of technological and regulatory change is set to continue throughout the 1990s. The most important changes will be:

■ **Fragmentation of broadcasting supply.** By 1996 there are likely to be 5 terrestrial television channels and at least 20 satellite and cable television channels aimed primarily at the U.K. market. On radio, there may be as many as 9 national and almost 200 local stations. All these services can be carried on transmission systems and frequencies that exist today. Beyond 1996, the anticipated introduction of digital compression on television and of digital audio broadcasting on radio will create the potential for even more channels and stations. Nobody can predict with any degree of certainty what will be the 'natural limit' of broadcasting supply in the U.K. What does seem clear is that we have not yet reached it.

■ **Fragmentation of broadcasting consumption.** As historical supply constraints are relaxed, increasing numbers of people will become accustomed to using a range of channels. The evidence from existing satellite and cable homes suggests that people will regularly watch 8-10 channels and listen to at least 2-3 radio stations. They will choose from a 'menu' of broadcasting services, picking out programmes which appeal to them, rather than remaining rigidly loyal to particular broadcasters. The increasing use of the video cassette recorder, audio taping equipment, compact disc technology and video games will further fragment the consumption of broadcasting services.

■ **Segmentation of the broadcasting market.** When the supply and consumption of broadcasting services was constrained, the BBC and its few competitors were able to reach the bulk of the audience on either television or radio with broadbased general entertainment services. But, as these constraints are relaxed and the number of channels increases, we can expect to see an increasing segmentation of the broadcasting market. There will continue to be some channels on television offering a broad schedule of light and general entertainment to large audiences. However, there will also be an increasing number of narrowly targeted specialist channels – primarily transmitted by satellite and cable television – with a much more direct appeal to particular groups amongst the viewing audience. Many of these new specialist channels will be accessible only to those who choose to and can afford to pay for them. Different groups of viewers will choose to purchase different packages of services. Meanwhile on radio, there will be a growing array of stations, although most of them will offer increasingly narrowly defined types of popular music.

■ **Growth in direct spending on broadcasting.** People will invest more and more money in broadcasting. This will enable the rapid takeup of satellite and cable services – already almost 3 million households have bought these services, and that figure has been increasing at the rate of roughly 85,000 per month. It may also enable further penetration of the latest broadcasting hardware and software – including quite possibly widescreen or high definition television equipment as it becomes available to the mass market. Over time, people will become increasingly aware of, and sympathetic to, a wide variety of ways of paying for broadcasting or related services – including for some of the services provided by the BBC. Their expenditure on broadcasting services will typically stretch to include not just the licence fee, but also subscription fees for satellite and cable channels, spending on video software and broadcasting related publications and consumer products.

■ **Redistribution of audience share.** The BBC used to have an almost guaranteed majority share of the broadcasting audience. Even today, it has a 45 per cent share of the television audience and a 60 per cent share of the radio audience. The average person watches or listens to BBC programmes for more than 20 hours a week. However, throughout the 1990s, we can expect to see a progressive redistribution of audience share between existing and new services. As the broadcasting market fragments, no single broadcaster will be able to sustain a dominant share of viewing or listening. Instead, audience share will be much more evenly spread across a range of broadcasting services. Television audiences will increasingly divide their viewing time between three distinct sectors of the broadcasting market – publicly funded broadcasting on the BBC; commercially funded broadcasting on ITV, Channel 4 and Channel 5; and commercially funded specialist channels on satellite and cable. Similarly, radio audiences will split their time between the BBC, national commercial broadcasting on INR, and local commercial broadcasting on ILR.

■ **Redistribution of industry revenues.** When the current Charter was issued in 1981, the licence fee provided the BBC with more than 50 per cent of the broadcasting industry's total revenue. By the end of the 1990s, however, the licence fee, if continued, would have fallen to between 25 and 30 per cent. Industry revenues would be almost equally divided between the licence fee, subscription fees and advertising revenue:

— **Subscription revenues for satellite and cable channels – primarily for movie and sport services – are predicted to grow rapidly to over £2 billion in real terms by the end of the decade.**

— **By that time, advertising revenue – which will probably grow at a much more modest rate – will also have increased to well over £2 billion.**

**Changing share of broadcasting industry revenues %**

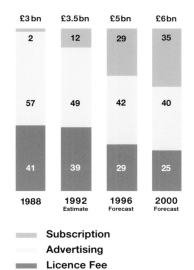

| | £3bn | £3.5bn | £5bn | £6bn |
|---|---|---|---|---|
| Subscription | 2 | 12 | 29 | 35 |
| Advertising | 57 | 49 | 42 | 40 |
| Licence Fee | 41 | 39 | 29 | 25 |
| | 1988 | 1992 Estimate | 1996 Forecast | 2000 Forecast |

- Subscription
- Advertising
- Licence Fee

Source: BBC Policy and Planning Unit

On these projections, roughly a third of total broadcasting industry revenue would be generated by advertising on mainstream commercial services; a further third would be generated by subscription fees for satellite and cable services; and a third or less would be generated by public funding.

**The broadcasting industry has begun to move towards a new structural model**

■ **Radical changes in broadcasting industry costs.** When the current Charter was issued in 1981, the BBC was part of a high cost industry. Throughout ITV and ILR as well as the BBC, costs were kept high by a combination of entrenched working practices, cumbersome organisation structures, over-staffing and poor industrial relations. In the last few years, this has started to change. The broadcasting industry has begun to move towards a new 'structural model'. Its principal elements are:

— The industry is characterised by increasing flexibility of employment practices and conditions, use of freelance and contracted staff, and mobility.

— A number of broadcasters are choosing to separate the management of their broadcasting, programme production and resource activities to ensure appropriate managerial focus and financial discipline in each activity.

— They are increasing the proportion of their television programming that is commissioned from independent producers, in order to reach the legislated minimum of 25 per cent by 1993.

— There is growing use of externally supplied contractual services at all levels of the industry.

The general effect of this new structural model is to enable the industry to exert much tighter control over the costs of broadcasting, programme production and resource management. As a result, many of the industry's costs have started to decline. However, other elements are actually increasing, driven upwards by fierce competitive pressure. For instance, the costs of high profile talent, the rights to sporting events and feature films are on a steep upward spiral. It seems likely that much of the cost saving generated by changes in working practices will be reinvested in acquiring the rights to high quality talent and programming.

■ **Reduced regulatory control of commercial services.** In the past, the BBC's commercial competitors were subject to tight public service regulation. The regulatory regime which governed ITV dictated a significant number of specific public service obligations and exercised strong control over the quality of commercial broadcasting. But for the rest of the 1990s, Channel 4 alone amongst commercial broadcasters will be tightly regulated. Both ITV and Channel 5 will be subject to lighter touch regulation by the ITC. INR and ILR will have a similarly light touch regime under the Radio Authority. Satellite channels on Astra will continue to be effectively free of regulatory control. Commercial broadcasters will thus have a much freer rein to maximise their audiences and revenues by whatever means they think best.

## 1

It is clear, therefore, that the broadcasting market of the 1990s will continue – and probably accelerate – the transformation of supply and demand that began in the 1980s. New technology and regulatory changes will further expand the number of channels available to viewers and listeners. Commercial priorities and objectives will become increasingly prominent in the broadcasting market, and there will be radical changes in the distribution of audience share and of industry revenues.

However, there is much that we do not know about the broadcasting environment of the 1990s and beyond. We do not, for instance, know what impact this proliferation will have on the choice and diversity of services available to viewers and listeners. Nor do we know what impact it will have on the provision of high quality but less commercially appealing programmes. Above all, we do not know for how long the broadcasting market in Britain will continue to be characterised by uncertainty and instability.

## GROWING INTERNATIONAL EXPERIENCE

This process of change is not unique to the U.K. Almost every developed country in the world has been going through a similar broadcasting revolution. In most cases, the causes of this revolution have been the same as in the U.K. – new technology and regulatory change. If anything, the U.K. is rather late in experiencing the effects of increased competition, audience fragmentation and new revenue sources that we are now starting to see. This gives us the chance to learn from what has happened elsewhere.

In most countries, the changing broadcasting environment has brought some important benefits. Where the number of television and radio channels has increased severalfold, some of the new channels have represented genuinely new types of service; new and existing broadcasters have competed more fiercely than ever before for audiences, revenues and reputation; and consumers have spent more and more money on broadcasting services, expanding – in some cases quite dramatically – the money available for the broadcasting industry to spend on programming. In many countries, broadcasting is one of the fastest growth service industries.

However, the experience has not all been positive. In many countries, the broadcasting revolution has brought many new channels, but all too often little extension in the real choice available; the economics of all but the most successful and powerful broadcasters have been shaky; and as a consequence there has been a marked reduction in the overall quality of programming throughout the broadcasting system. Only in Japan has a sustainable role and funding regime been established for high quality public service broadcasting at the heart of the broadcasting system.

■ **In the U.S.**, for example, the average household can now receive 50 or more television channels and about as many radio stations. Competition between these services is intense, but it is focused almost entirely on the battle for ratings, share and revenues between extremely aggressive commercial operators.

**Commercial priorities will become increasingly prominent in the broadcasting market**

— Some of the newer specialist channels on cable television have started to make important contributions to public service broadcasting. CNN in news, Discovery in factual programming, and Arts and Entertainment in drama have generated or acquired programming of distinction and quality. However, each of these channels individually reaches a relatively small audience – on average around 1 per cent of households – and their programming remains very much oriented towards making a profit.

— The principal burden of supplying high quality broadcasting for the mainstream audience continues to fall on the three networks (ABC, CBS and NBC) – now supplemented by the emerging Fox Network. That burden has proved increasingly difficult to bear as network economics have deteriorated in the face of competition from cable television, and investment in programme quality has been cut back. Last year, two out of the three major networks lost money, and all three made substantial reductions in programming costs, with the greatest impact on news coverage and drama programming.

— In these circumstances, the role of the main public service broadcasting network (PBS) has been relegated to what is frequently referred to as a 'cultural ghetto'. It is funded primarily by commercial sponsorship, private donations and very limited congressional grants. As a consequence, it is able to afford only specialist or cultural programming with limited audience appeal – much of it imported since there are insufficient funds for original programming. As a result, its ability to offer high quality programming of U.S. origin to a broad audience is severely restricted.

■ **In France,** the main public service broadcaster (TF 1) was privatised in the mid-1980s, and has since pursued a very successful strategy of commercial programming to maximise its audience ratings and share. Its commercial success has been paralleled by the increasing strength of Canal Plus, a subscriber-funded movies and sport channel. However, these have been the only two channels which have benefited from deregulation in France. The others, whether terrestrial, satellite or cable, have consistently lost money and one – La Cinq – has recently declared bankruptcy. The remaining public service broadcasters – recently renamed France 2 and France 3 – have struggled to generate sufficient funds from a combination of advertising and public funding to cover a full programming schedule. Both channels have lost a substantial share of the audience and of industry revenues, and are increasingly unable to play a pivotal role in the development of original French programming. Their future plans for amalgamation are evidence of their problems.

■ **In Germany**, also with a terrestrial, cable and satellite mix, the commercial channels – Sat 1 and RTL Plus – have pursued similarly aggressive commercial strategies to that pioneered by TF 1. They have built audiences and revenues on the back of highly populist programming. The public service broadcasters – ARD and ZDF – who are both required to generate advertising revenue to supplement licence fee funds, have found it increasingly difficult to compete. They have also lost share of

**In many countries there has been a marked reduction in the quality of programming**

audience and revenues, and their influence on the quality of German broadcasting has markedly decreased.

■ **In Australia,** the main public service broadcaster (ABC) now has a very limited budget, granted directly out of government funds, and a similarly limited broadcasting remit. Its share of the broadcasting audience is less than 20 per cent. Broadcasting in Australia is dominated by the three main commercial networks (Channels 7, 9 and 10), each of which has been in bankruptcy within the last few years, with inevitable consequences for programme quality.

■ **In Canada,** the main public service broadcaster (CBC) has been adversely affected by government funding pressures. Its grant from government now covers only 65 per cent of its operating costs. In an effort to plug the funding gap with commercial revenue, CBC has been forced to dilute its reputation for programme quality. Its share of the audience has fallen to around 15 per cent and English-speaking television has become increasingly affected by 'overspill' from the neighbouring U.S. There is a growing awareness of the potential threat to Canadian culture from the progressive weakening of CBC's market position.

■ **Only in Japan** does there appear to have been a concentrated effort to sustain a viable long term future for public service broadcasting. The main Japanese public service broadcaster, NHK, is able to meet most of the costs of its two television channels and radio stations with licence fee funds – covering a full commitment to news, educational and cultural programming. In addition, NHK has been granted permission to establish two satellite services – one focused on news programming and the other on general programming – and to generate subscription funds from those services. With this mixed funding base and a clear programming mandate, NHK's combination of terrestrial and satellite public service channels remains at the heart of Japanese broadcasting.

**The combination of terrestrial and satellite public service channels remains at the heart of Japanese broadcasting**

• • •

**In summary, the broadcasting environment in the U.K. is going through a period of radical change. The Old World in which the BBC's traditional role and services were developed has passed into history. In the New World, there will be more broadcasters, more television and radio channels, and more choice for viewers and listeners. However, there will also be more risks, more uncertainties and more sources of instability in the broadcasting system. It is against this background that we have questioned the role and services of the BBC and the best way to fund and account for it in the future.**

# A Clear Public Purpose for the BBC 2

— **a clear role**

— **extending choice**

— **access for all**

— **high quality programmes**

The substantial changes that are taking place in the broadcasting environment clearly justify a thorough reassessment of the BBC and of public service broadcasting in the U.K. That reassessment should ask whether there will be the need for a publicly funded broadcasting organisation such as the BBC in the broadcasting market of the mid-1990s – and if so what specific public purpose it should be required to meet.

The BBC's Charter Review process has addressed these questions, and this Chapter summarises its conclusions.

## DO WE NEED THE BBC?

Some people may take the view that by the mid-1990s a public service broadcasting organisation funded by a mandatory licence fee will be an anomaly, because:

- The commercially funded market for broadcasting services will be fully developed, and there will be no need to reinforce or supplement the market with publicly funded services.

- Viewers and listeners will be able to choose from a multiplicity of commercial television and radio services, offering a much extended range of choice.

- Many of these commercial services will offer at least some programming of high quality – including programmes with specialist appeal.

- The commercial market will be well funded by a combination of advertising and voluntary subscription fees paid directly by consumers.

**Commercially funded broadcasters and publicly funded broadcasters have different, but complementary, objectives**

What these arguments fail to reflect, however, is that commercially funded broadcasters and publicly funded broadcasters have different, but complementary, objectives – and that both have a role to play in ensuring a healthy and robust broadcasting system.

- **Commercially funded broadcasters** quite properly set their priorities for programming and services against the overriding need to make a profit and generate a return for their shareholders. That is their obligation as commercial organisations. Within the constraints of their contractual obligations to regulators, and their own concern for the public interest, these priorities require them to broadcast programmes that attract large or commercially attractive audiences; to schedule them in such a way as to maintain those audiences; and to limit their investment in programming to what the commercial market will afford.

- **Publicly funded broadcasters**, in contrast, have a primary obligation to the public. They do not need to make a profit nor generate a return to shareholders. Their overriding public purpose is to extend choice by guaranteeing access for everyone in the country to programming services that are of unusually high quality and that are, or might be, at risk in the purely commercially funded sector of the market.

## 2

The international experience outlined in Chapter 1 suggests that countries which allow the balance to shift too strongly in favour of one or other type of broadcasting have less real choice and/or reduced quality in their broadcasting services. In particular, a purely commercial market is naturally dominated by programming and services aimed at making a profit by attracting large or commercially attractive audiences. Programming with a clear public purpose but without the ability to make money is kept to a minimum and often pushed to the margins of the schedule.

However, the balance between the services supplied by publicly funded broadcasting and commercially funded broadcasting will change over time – particularly during a period of radical change in the commercial broadcasting market. The rapid expansion of commercially funded broadcasting services through the 1990s will not invalidate the need for publicly funded broadcasting; but it will serve more clearly to limit and to define the specific role that it should play in pursuit of its public purpose.

In the past, as a dominant provider, the BBC had an obligation to cover all audiences and broadcasting needs; in the future it will have an obligation to focus on performing a set of clearly defined roles that best complement the enlarged commercial sector. In our view, there are four such roles:

- **Providing the comprehensive, in-depth and impartial news and information coverage across a range of broadcasting outlets that is needed to support a fair and informed national debate.**

- **Supporting and stimulating the development and expression of British culture and entertainment.**

- **Guaranteeing the provision of programming and services that create opportunities for education.**

- **Stimulating the communication of cultures and ideas between Britain and abroad.**

The BBC should pursue its primary roles through the distinctiveness and quality of its own output; through the way that it structures its programme schedules; and through the standards that it sets for itself and for the whole industry. It should evolve and adapt its services to deliver these roles and objectives. Over time, it should withdraw from programme areas or types in which it is no longer able or needed to make an original contribution

What then are the defining characteristics of the BBC's public purpose?

## INFORMING THE NATIONAL DEBATE

**Firstly, the BBC should aim to provide the comprehensive, in-depth and impartial news and information coverage across a range of broadcasting outlets that is needed to support a fair and informed national debate.**

Nobody could or would wish to make the argument that a purely commercial market would be devoid of informative news and current affairs programming.

**In the future
the BBC will focus
on performing
a set of clearly
defined roles**

Commercial broadcasters in this country and abroad have proud track records of informing their audiences both on television and radio.

However, there are strong reasons for believing that a purely commercial market would offer a more limited range of news, information and analysis. In such a market, there would be strong commercial pressures on broadcasters to:

- Concentrate on a relatively narrow range of issues with proven commercial appeal.

- Focus on the domestic side of the news agenda with an emphasis on human interest stories in order to capture large audiences.

- Limit the analysis and debate of complex and demanding issues that may be of great importance to the country but that sometimes make for less popular programming.

- Tailor news and information coverage and resources to the need to make a profit.

- Schedule current affairs programming with limited commercial appeal outside peak time.

**To ensure that issues of importance to the nation, irrespective of immediate popular commercial appeal, will be properly reported, debated and analysed**

For instance, in recent years commercial pressures have forced the U.S. television networks to cut their overseas news coverage resources and to focus on a much 'softer' news agenda at home. In the U.K., commercial pressures have radically reduced the scope of the news coverage available on independent radio, and the future role of current affairs programmes on U.K. commercial television is very much in doubt, with strong pressures emerging to move current affairs and other factual programming out of prime time.

A fully rounded and informed public awareness of issues of national importance will therefore continue to depend in part on the news and information coverage provided by publicly funded broadcasting. It should therefore be a core role of the BBC to help inform the British public, and in doing so:

- To maintain the highest standards of independence, impartiality and responsibility in its reporting.

- To ensure that issues of importance to the nation, irrespective of immediate popular commercial appeal, will be properly reported, debated and analysed.

- To provide universal access through local, regional, national and international outlets to the broadest range of issues, voices and styles.

- To ensure an appropriate mix of coverage of international, national and regional issues and perspectives.

- To deliver comprehensive coverage of the political process, including Parliament, party conferences and national and local elections.

- To provide a broad base of knowledge and understanding through documentaries, consumer and other factual programmes.

## EXPRESSING BRITISH CULTURE AND ENTERTAINMENT

**Secondly, the BBC should support and stimulate the development and expression of British culture and entertainment.**

This encompasses a broad range of cultural and entertainment programmes, from those with a sustained appeal to large audiences, to those that interest only relatively small groups. It certainly does not imply an exclusive focus on 'high culture'; but it does imply a commitment to reflect and nurture the U.K.'s rich cultural heritage.

This again, is not something that the BBC can expect to do alone. Many commercial broadcasters, including ITV and Channel 4, have strong traditions of innovative and high quality cultural and entertainment programming. They, along with the newer commercial channels on television and radio, will continue to entertain large audiences and to express important dimensions of our culture.

Nevertheless, overseas and domestic experience reveals that assigning cultural and entertainment programming exclusively to a purely commercial broadcasting market results in overriding commercial pressures to:

■ Produce, schedule and broadcast only programmes that can be relied upon to attract large audiences.

■ Concentrate, in particular, on producing easily digestible entertainment within well established formats.

■ Schedule programmes which innovate primarily outside peak viewing and listening times, if at all.

■ Produce or import a significant quantity of programmes as cheaply as possible and 'in bulk' as a response to commercial cost pressures.

■ Play safe and limit investment in programmes that take risks.

■ Rapidly abandon programmes which are not an instant ratings success.

■ Focus radio services on the pop and popular music markets, and minimise higher cost speech content.

The BBC can play a critical role in countering the risk that these will become the defining characteristics of British broadcasting – as they have in other countries. It should, therefore, be a core role of the BBC to reflect the full and diverse range of culture and entertainment in modern British society. It should seek in particular:

■ To portray all forms of entertainment, humour, artistic and cultural expression.

■ To reflect all the dimensions of both popular and minority culture that make us different as a nation.

■ To give special prominence to the artistic, sporting and ceremonial events that bring the nation together.

**To reflect the full and diverse range of culture and entertainment in modern British society**

- To be an active cultural patron – fostering and nurturing the national talents, originating and commissioning new works and developing excellence in the arts.

- To take risks with innovative programming.

- To portray a multiracial, multicultural society and to respond to the diversity of cultures throughout the U.K.

- To schedule its programmes so that these priorities are reflected in prime time viewing and listening hours when large audiences are available.

## CREATING OPPORTUNITIES FOR EDUCATION

**Thirdly, the BBC should guarantee the provision of programming and services that create opportunities for education.**

Much of the programming produced by commercial broadcasters has educative value for its audience, but education is not a primary role and objective of most commercial broadcasters. A purely commercial market would be highly unlikely to cater adequately for the public's need and desire for programmes and services which help to educate them. We have observed that:

- Commercial markets do not deliver a full range of educational and educative services because they lack broad popular and commercial appeal.

- Yet there is a demand in all parts of British society for more education and training for people of all ages, using all the means of communication available.

- Broadcasting services, in conjunction with other media, have the potential to play an important role in the formal educational system, applying the latest technology to reach and communicate with people.

- Those same broadcasting media can contribute to people's broader education through programmes of all types which have educative value for their audiences and which broaden horizons for all.

We therefore believe that it should be a core role of the BBC to provide educative programming in all its services and genres. Its particular objectives should be:

- To increase the insights, understanding and knowledge of its audience across the full range of its programming.

- To support and reinforce the formal educational process and thus contribute to the development of a 'learning society'.

- To include within a mixed schedule for large prime time audiences a substantial output of science, arts, history, literature and music programming which creates opportunities for education.

**To increase the insights, understanding and knowledge of its audience across the full range of its programming**

- **To provide training and vocational services which allow the individual to develop fully.**

- **To reflect insights and perspectives on the rest of the world to this country.**

COMMUNICATING BETWEEN THE U.K. AND ABROAD

**Fourthly, the BBC should also play a role as one of the primary means of communication between the U.K. and other countries. It should bring credit to the U.K. around the world, and promote understanding of British culture and values.**

Commercial broadcasters participate vigorously in the international broadcasting market through programme sales and co-productions. There are also a growing number of international broadcasting companies who have a commercial presence in several broadcasting markets around the world.

However, the BBC is the only British broadcaster with the resources, experience and worldwide standing to deliver a coherent range of radio, television and other programme services to overseas audiences. The BBC's success in international broadcasting is founded upon:

- **Impartiality, rooted in the independence and objectivity of the BBC's domestic services.**

- **Accuracy, made possible by the BBC's depth of journalistic resources and specialist expertise, both at home and abroad.**

- **Quality, reflecting the BBC's commitment to producing programmes of the highest standards across all genres.**

World Service Radio is the world's most trusted and listened-to international source of news and information, culture and entertainment, and the much younger World Service Television has already established a major presence in international television broadcasting. The volume of the BBC's programme sales and co-productions is such that the BBC is now the biggest single distributor in international broadcasting.

This unequalled range of international activities serves the national interest by promoting understanding of British culture and democratic values, enriching people's lives and bringing credit to the U.K. It also serves the national interest by underpinning a substantial export industry. British television has been one of the U.K.'s most successful export industries, and the BBC itself has had a substantially positive 'balance of payments'. It continues to do so, even while the broadcasting industry as a whole substantially increases its level of imports.

The BBC has built up a 'virtuous circle' of domestic quality underpinning international exports, which in turn help to pay for domestic programme making of the highest quality. Up to 10 per cent of the BBC's television schedule is now supported by funds generated from international programme sales and co-productions.

For these reasons, it should be a core role of the BBC to provide programming services of value and distinction to overseas audiences, as well as to reflect foreign

**The world's most trusted international source of news and information, culture and entertainment**

cultures and perspectives in its services to the British audience. In particular, it should:

- Sustain and build **World Service Radio** which, as the acknowledged provider of global information, should continue to reflect the U.K. to the world, and the world to itself. Although funded by grant-in-aid from the Foreign and Commonwealth Office (FCO), its overall authority, credibility and editorial independence, as well as the richness of its news resources, will continue to be derived from, and assured by, its position as an integral part of the BBC.

- Build up **World Service Television**, employing to the full the capability of satellite television to reach international audiences.

- Increase the already substantial volume of BBC programme sales and co-productions, using new programming and archive material to extend the exposure and reach of British broadcasting.

- Reflect international developments and perspectives to the British audience through its full range of programming – taking full advantage of the contribution that the World Service makes to the BBC's international reputation, access and infrastructure.

● ● ●

This chapter has set out a clear public purpose for the BBC in the new broadcasting environment of the 1990s and beyond. It has argued that a publicly funded broadcaster such as the BBC is needed in order to guarantee universal access to some of the most important broadcasting services and benefits that are, or might be, at risk in a purely commercial broadcasting market. With this as its objective, the BBC of the 1990s should offer a range of distinctive, high quality programming services in each of the major genres.

We have considered the arguments of those who suggest that the BBC should focus only on providing services that meet the minority needs of smaller audiences – needs that clearly will not be met in the commercial market. These people suggest that any programme or service which attracts a large audience could be adequately supplied by the commercial market – and should not, therefore, be publicly funded.

However, to go down this route would be to preclude the majority of licence payers from viewing and listening to programmes and services which they value and appreciate. It would be to force publicly funded broadcasting in the U.K. into the kind of 'cultural ghetto' which has so weakened the broadcasting system in the U.S., Australia and elsewhere. It would also be to limit quite unnecessarily the contribution that publicly funded broadcasting can make through the BBC to quality standards in broadcasting across the full range of programming.

The BBC should therefore maintain regular contact with all viewers and listeners, and deliver programming which appeals to them. It should provide value through its services to as many people as possible. But it should do so in a way which places the

**The BBC should maintain regular contact with all viewers and listeners**

greatest importance on developing services of distinction and quality, rather than on attracting a large audience for its own sake.

This is a creative challenge which the BBC, by virtue of its traditions, culture and aspirations, is well placed to tackle. But its pursuit of this challenge should not be taken merely on trust. The BBC should explain very clearly how it will pursue its objectives through its programmes and the way it organises its affairs. The next two chapters therefore outline how the BBC should fashion its programmes and services to achieve its objectives in the much changed broadcasting market of the 1990s.

# High Quality Programmes

**3**

— impartial news and information

— programmes that innovate,
  challenge and entertain

— a strategy for education

— bringing credit to the U.K.

G iven the roles set out in Chapter 2, what specific types of programmes should the BBC make and broadcast? What should be the characteristics that distinguish BBC programmes and schedules from those of other broadcasters? Through what range of broadcasting services should the BBC deliver these programmes to the viewing and listening audience?

We have explored each of these questions through a fundamental reappraisal of the BBC's programme and service strategies. We have interrogated:

■ The viewers and listeners – exploring their views through an extensive programme of research and asking what they will want and need from BBC programmes in the future.

■ The broadcasting environment – asking what other broadcasters are offering, what they will offer in the future, and in what – if any – respects they will fail to deliver what viewers and listeners want and need.

■ The creative opportunities – asking what creative skills and ideas the BBC can offer in each programme area, and how these skills and ideas can best be deployed to give viewers and listeners what they want and need of the BBC.

**A set of preferred strategies for the BBC in each programme area**

From this enquiry we have drawn up a set of preferred strategies for the BBC in each programme area. Some of these strategies represent a marked change of direction, in response to the changing environment. Others are more of a continuation or enhancement of existing strategies which – after review – still seem appropriate for the future.

This chapter outlines the principal characteristics of the BBC's preferred strategy in each programme area and shows how they relate directly to the four elements of its public purpose.

INFORMING THE NATIONAL DEBATE

Throughout its history, and particularly in recent years, the BBC has made an important contribution to informing the British public. Its achievements in news, current affairs and information programming are unmatched by other broadcasters, in this country or overseas.

The BBC has recognised the pivotal importance of this role and the public appetite for information. While other broadcasters have been forced by commercial pressures to cut back their news coverage, the BBC has made a strategic investment in news and current affairs.

It has invested in the authority and expertise of its journalism, recognising that the fundamental requirements of public service information programming are to ensure accuracy, impartiality and clear analysis. It has employed more specialist correspondents; increased its investment in newsgathering resources at regional, national and international levels; extended the range and variety of news and current affairs programmes on television and radio; built a formidable strand of feature and documentary programming on both television and radio; and focused local radio on high quality local journalism and information.

At the same time, the BBC has aimed for the highest possible level of productivity. It has formed a single News and Current Affairs directorate covering both radio and television and a single, multiskilled newsgathering operation. It has extended its unique network of joint radio and television foreign bureaux; and it has introduced joint radio and television newsgathering at the regional level. These initiatives have increased the BBC's ability to inform the public accurately, quickly and with improved value for money.

This strategy has already achieved results. Over 20 million people a day now watch BBC television news and 10 million listen to BBC radio news. Research shows that over two thirds of the population consider the BBC the best broadcasting service for news, and nearly 70 per cent consider the BBC highly trustworthy, as against 33 per cent for their daily newspaper.

However, the BBC faces new and substantial challenges if it is to maintain and even enhance its contribution in the news and information area. In the new broadcasting environment people will demand much more of their information providers. In addition to regular news bulletins at fixed times, they will expect continuously available news to match their increasingly flexible schedules. They will require immediate 'on the scene' coverage of major events – whether scheduled or unscheduled. And they will assign greatest trust to those broadcasters who, as well as editing and analysing the news for them, also deliver it 'unprocessed'.

The BBC can best meet these new challenges by pursuing five key programme strategies:

■ **Continuous improvement of news and information programmes.** The BBC should push ahead with the next phase of its strategy to enhance the quality of its news and information programmes on television and radio. It should:

— **Further increase the quality of its radio and television journalism, extend the reach of its foreign bureau network and intensify the use of multiskilled field teams across both media.**

— **Enhance the coverage of both Westminster and the European Parliament.**

— **Strengthen weekend news services on television and radio.**

— **Upgrade the Ceefax service as more and more people use teletext as a primary source of news and information.**

■ **Development of continuous news services.** It is becoming clear that regularly scheduled news bulletins and current affairs programmes alone cannot meet the increasing information needs and expectations of audiences. With partial exposure to CNN and/or Sky News, as well as to the BBC's own News FM radio service during the Gulf War, the public now expects to be kept directly in touch with breaking news, particularly at times of crisis. Meeting these expectations should be a public service priority for the BBC. It can only do this by delivering continuous news channels on radio and television, applying the experience and skills of BBC journalists and the breadth of its newsgathering coverage to deliver truly distinctive services.

**BBC's news and current affairs reputation**

% of population who believe that...

the BBC provides a high quality news service

87%

the BBC is the best national news provider

67%

Source: BBC Corporate Image Survey, 1992.

**News and information programmes**

General Election 1992
BBC 1

Gulf War
BBC 1

**Panorama**
BBC 1

**Newsnight**
BBC 2

**Today Programme**
Radio 4

**Midlands Today**
BBC Birmingham

It should, therefore, be a strategic priority for the BBC to:

— **Deliver a continuous news service on radio, building on and extending the news platform established by Radio 4. The BBC has announced that such a service will be launched in 1994.**

— **Participate in the development of a continuous news service on satellite and cable television, drawing on the existing journalistic resources of News and Current Affairs and the World Service.**

■ **Further enhancement of current affairs output.** It is already clear that a commitment to current affairs programming will increasingly be a distinguishing feature of BBC television and radio. While other broadcasters may push current affairs programming to the margins of the schedule, or avoid it altogether, the BBC should maintain it at the heart of the peak time schedule on both television and radio. It should broadcast a range of daily reports, weekly and monthly reviews, and periodic coverage of major issues, national and international events. Across the range of its current affairs programming, the BBC should:

— **Focus its journalistic resources on in-depth reporting, investigation, analysis and interpretation of the main issues of the day.**

— **Provide the information and airtime to debate the most important and broad ranging issues of the moment in-depth across both radio and television.**

— **Further extend its coverage of European issues and cultures, to reflect the growing importance of the European agenda.**

— **Open up the current affairs output to independent producers in order to extend the range of the in-house agenda.**

■ **Further enhancement of regional journalism.** The BBC should reinforce its commitment to delivering high quality local and regional journalism on both television and radio. There is an increasing array of stories and issues that may not be included on the network radio and television agendas, but which are high on the agenda of regional audiences and have a direct and far-reaching effect on people's lives. Audience research shows how highly people value authoritative news coverage of local events and issues. The BBC should respond to this challenge by:

— **Concentrating its local and regional services across both media on in-depth reporting and analysis of key issues, using specialist expertise in its journalism.**

— **Delivering an increasingly high quality daily regional television news service, supported by weekly current affairs and parliamentary programmes across the year.**

— **Basing its local radio services on speech and information, delivering a consistently high quality of journalism 7 days a week. As ILR becomes overwhelmingly music focused, the BBC should complete its transition to primarily speech based local radio, offering a comprehensive source of local news and information.**

■ **Further extension to the range of investigative and reflective information programming.** In addition to the regular daily and weekly cycle of news and current affairs, the BBC should be committed to a wider range of information programmes. The BBC has unique specialist expertise in making programmes that increase the audience's understanding of the world around them – through regular magazine programmes, specialist and general series and one-off documentaries. The BBC should apply that expertise across the television and radio schedule to:

— Investigate the social, economic and cultural issues and themes in our society and in other societies.

— Involve viewers and listeners in programmes which address challenges to society including crime, homelessness, drug addiction and public health.

— Maintain a regular flow of information, advice and support to consumers, particularly through investigative reporting of commercial malpractice.

— Explore and explain the issues confronting business and commerce, and identify how they will affect the public at large.

— Chronicle modern and contemporary history – both political and social – through original research and creative use of the BBC's archive.

— Pioneer forms of 'access television and radio', ranging from local radio community programming to social action broadcasting on television and radio.

## EXPRESSING BRITISH CULTURE AND ENTERTAINMENT

The BBC has an equally strong track record in creating and developing broadcasting services which nurture and express British culture and entertainment. Across a broad spectrum of cultural and entertainment genres, it has developed programming of the highest quality. As a consequence, the BBC has consistently won large audiences, industry awards and critical and international acclaim for its drama, comedy, children's programming, religious output, sports coverage and music and arts programming.

This track record has demonstrated that there is no essential conflict between entertaining an audience and delivering high quality programmes. The BBC's public purpose is compatible with, indeed is dependent upon, engaging and entertaining the audience. The creative challenge for the BBC is to deliver programmes that innovate, challenge **and** entertain.

However, the transformation of the broadcasting environment requires the BBC to take a fundamental look at its cultural and entertainment programming in the context of the wide array of services that will increasingly be available in the commercial marketplace.

In the new broadcasting environment, many television viewers will have access to commercial services which provide an extensive diet of popular drama, light

**Investigative and reflective information programming**

**You and Yours**
Radio 4

**Troubleshooter**
BBC 2

**Churchill**
BBC 1

**Drama programming**

Kenneth Branagh's Hamlet
Radio 3

Clarissa
BBC 2

Edge of Darkness
BBC 2

Casualty
BBC 1

entertainment and comedy; which carry some factual and dramatic programmes of quality and appeal; and which supply a much enlarged volume of movies, sport and pop music. Radio listeners will have access to services which meet the particular music listening needs of their audiences much more precisely than before.

In these circumstances, the BBC's task should be to provide a range and quality of cultural and entertainment programming which extends choice in the marketplace. It should invest in the kinds of programming which it is uniquely equipped to do well – and eschew programming of a type and quality that can be found in abundance elsewhere. With this as the overall objective, the BBC's cultural and entertainment strategy should:

■ **Restore the BBC's place as the primary focus of broadcast drama** – from the point of view of producers and directors, writers, actors and, above all, audiences. The BBC should be the 'National Theatre of the Airwaves'. It should extend the volume, range and styles of drama output on television, and it should build on BBC Radio's unique role as the biggest commissioner of drama in the world. BBC drama on television and radio should aim to:

— Ensure a coherent and planned output of classic plays, which over time will provide every viewer and listener with access to the theatrical works of the great dramatists of our culture – from Shakespeare and Jonson to Shaw and Osborne.

— Provide a similarly planned output of classic literary adaptations, which over time will ensure frequent and regular exposure to the great works of writers such as Dickens, Conrad, Trollope and George Eliot.

— Invest in the commissioning of original drama – through single plays, films, serials or series – which attract the best contemporary talents to television and radio.

— Maintain a consistent stream of modern literary adaptations, drawing upon the work of our best living authors.

— Sustain a commitment to continuous drama series which accurately reflect and chronicle British society past and present in a way that is realistic, topical, thought provoking and entertaining.

— Guarantee to the British public that they will regularly be able to see and hear the work of our most talented actors and directors, in productions commissioned or adapted by the BBC.

— Create an effective partnership between television and radio to commission, support and stimulate new writers and new performers.

— Reflect the full cultural diversity of the country – with regular dramatic contributions from regional and national regional centres and the commissioning of new work by writers and producers from ethnic communities.

— Supplement directly commissioned drama with coherent strands of feature films, which represent the best of world cinema – contemporary and of the past.

— Ensure that acquired international drama – whether in the form of plays, films, mini-series or series – matches the high quality of the BBC's own drama productions. Such programming should be acquired to extend the breadth and diversity of the BBC's drama output rather than to fill gaps in the schedule with cheap material.

The emphasis in this strategy should be on high quality drama programming which entertains its audience. The size of that audience will vary depending on the breadth of appeal that a particular drama programme achieves. BBC drama can and should be popular – but it should also consistently meet the highest quality standards and not simply be motivated by the search for large audiences.

■ **Carve out a unique role as the principal innovator and pioneer in comedy and light entertainment.** Innovation, creativity and quality should be the defining characteristics of the BBC's comedy and light entertainment programming. The BBC should make a joint investment across radio and television to develop fresh and unusual material that will capture the audience's imagination and reflect the best of the BBC's creative strengths. Those strengths should be applied to:

— Develop and extend the situation comedy format, which has genuinely contributed to the formation of the national culture by commenting on British life through humour.

— Generate, in particular, an expanded output on television of longer form (e.g, 50 minutes or more) comedy drama strands, which give greater freedom to the talents of major scriptwriters.

— Provide a platform for the best established and new comic performers, allowing time for them to grow on their audiences as others have before them.

— Develop new and fresh light entertainment formats.

— Stimulate the development of unusual and challenging quiz programming which tests the imagination and creativity of its audience.

— Develop strands of factually based entertainment formats, which cover leisure and popular culture – fashion, collecting, leisure pastimes, films and so on – with wit and imagination.

Within this strategy of innovation and creativity, there should be no room on the BBC's airwaves for derivative, 'formula' comedy or entertainment formats; nor for simple and unchallenging game shows and people shows which will be provided in abundance on other channels; nor for any entertainment programming which belittles or humiliates performers or members of the public.

■ **Provide a unique range of programmes for children and young people.** The BBC should invest to retain its position as the leading provider of the fullest range and highest standards of programmes for children and young people, delivered in a commercial

## Comedy and light entertainment programming

**Only Fools and Horses**
BBC 1

**Have I Got News For You**
BBC 2

**Mary Whitehouse Experience**
Radio 1 / BBC 2

## Children's and young people's programming

**Chronicles of Narnia**
BBC 1

**Newsround**
BBC 1

**Rough Guides**
BBC 2

## Music and arts programming

**Summer XS**
Radio 1

**Last Night of the Proms**
BBC 1/Radio 3

free environment. It should address children and young people through information, entertainment and educative programming, and in particular it should aim to:

— Provide an extended Sunday schedule of children's television, with a varied range of programming on Sunday morning, and a sustained commitment to the children's drama serial on Sunday afternoon.

— Deliver a broad stream of informational and educative programming especially designed for, and of appeal to, young people – including regular coverage of news and current affairs, travel, careers, fashion and social issues.

By and large, the BBC should concentrate its investment in children's programming on television, which is the most likely way of reaching children. There should be rather less drama and other programming on radio aimed primarily at children, since it generally fails to reach its target audience. But the BBC should apply its creative skills to developing strands of speech based radio entertainment, including stories and adaptations, that will be of interest to families and young people.

In following this strategy for children's programmes, there should be little room on the BBC for television programmes with an over-reliance on imported material or nonstop cartoons.

■ **Intensify its commitment to performance and coverage of music and the arts.** BBC radio and television should provide a uniquely rich diet of music and the arts. There should be live performance, indepth analysis and reportage, much new work and programmes made with a spirit of adventure and excitement. These characteristics should apply equally to the coverage of youth-oriented pop culture and to high culture. The BBC's music and arts programming should aim to:

— Emphasise live performance by consistent coverage of classical concerts, opera, ballet and rock concerts, and by in-depth coverage of music and arts festivals throughout the U.K., including the BBC Promenade Concerts and the Edinburgh Festival.

— Commission and broadcast new work, in order to stimulate and provide expression for the talents of composers, writers, musicians, artists and dancers.

— Extend the range of music available in commercial concert halls and through commercial broadcasting outlets – particularly through the work of the BBC's five orchestras and the BBC Singers.

— Create a partnership with the major national artistic institutions – the leading galleries, museums, theatre companies, opera houses and concert halls – to ensure the continuous provision of outstanding work, and to supplement it with authoritative coverage and analysis.

— Develop additional strands of artistic programming with a specifically educative dimension, ranging from music master classes and competitions for young writers, composers and performers, to programmes which chronicle and celebrate the history of our culture.

— **Maintain and build long running and continuous strands of arts magazine programming which cover the latest developments in music and the arts in a topical and informative way – using a variety of styles.**

The pursuit of this strategy for music programming will leave little or no room for radio programmes which consist of nonstop Top 40 music.

Young Musician of the Year
BBC 2

■ **Serve the national audience for sport with authoritative and creative approaches to coverage.** The BBC will be the only U.K. broadcaster providing a full range of sports to a national audience, free of commercial breaks. The primary elements of its sports strategy should be to:

— **Maintain the highest standards of sports coverage on television and radio. A critical dimension of the BBC's continued participation in the broadcasting of sport is the unique quality of its coverage. In all sports, and particularly in those major sports in which alternatives are available, the BBC should aim to deliver pictures, commentary, analysis and reportage of the highest standard. It should also aim to underpin its coverage with incisive sports journalism which meets the needs of both the sports enthusiast and the occasional viewer and listener.**

— **Ensure that major sporting events of national and international importance are covered on BBC television and radio. The BBC seeks to cover those major sporting events – Wimbledon, Test Match Cricket, The Boat Race, The FA and SFA Cup Finals, The Open Golf and so on – that unite the nation.**

— **Use the ability to schedule across two television channels and radio to make available full coverage of major sporting events. The role of radio will be particularly critical not just in maintaining national institutions like 'Test Match Special', but also in guaranteeing universal access to a range of sports.**

— **Maintain coverage of a range of sports – only a publicly funded broadcaster will maintain the coverage and exposure on which so many smaller sports depend.**

At a time of spiralling costs for sports contracts, the BBC must ensure that licence payers' money is spent judiciously in achieving these objectives. Its football partnership with BSkyB is an example of just such an approach. It allows the BBC to provide a full diet of recorded and live football – including the FA Cup, England internationals, the World Cup and weekly coverage of the Premier League – at a manageable cost.

## **Sports programming**

Olympics
BBC 1 / BBC 2

Desmond Lynam at Wimbledon
BBC 1/BBC 2

Test Match Special
Radio 3

## CREATING OPPORTUNITIES FOR EDUCATION

Education is one of the core roles of publicly funded broadcasting. The BBC has always recognised this fact, and has actively embraced its role in the formal and informal education of the nation. Charter Review has provided an opportunity for the BBC to reassess its educative programmes, and to set out a new strategic vision for the future.

**Educational programming and services**

School children using
BBC Education material

**Most popular school television series in primary schools**

| | | |
|---|---|---|
| 1 | Word and Pictures | BBC |
| 2 | Watch | BBC |
| 3 | Look and Read | BBC |
| 4 | Zig Zag | BBC |
| 5 | Landmarks | BBC |
| 6 | Thinkabout Science | BBC |
| 7 | How We Used to Live | ITV |
| 8 | Storytime | BBC |
| 9 | Maths Is Fun | ITV |
| 10 | Seeing and Doing | ITV |

Source: Survey of Viewing and Listening, 1991.

There is no doubting the impact of the BBC's contribution to formal education. Research has shown that 95 per cent of primary schools and 93 per cent of secondary schools make regular use of BBC Schools Television, and 77 per cent of primary schools use BBC Schools Radio. Two thirds of teachers regard BBC Schools broadcasts as central or useful to their teaching of the National Curriculum.

The BBC's partnership with the Open University has contributed to over 100,000 people gaining degrees. The BBC's long term commitment to Continuing Education has provided critical support for national initiatives to enhance adult literacy and numeracy, parent education, vocational skills, foreign language training and caring for the elderly.

The BBC has not seen its educative role as confined solely to support for formal education. It has also maintained a consistent stream of 'educative' programming in its general schedules on television and radio. This programming on science, history, religion, culture and current affairs makes new areas of knowledge available to a public who do not have access to it elsewhere.

The need for the BBC to do this and more in the future is clear. Society is attaching ever-increasing importance to education and training as a vital factor in our economic and cultural development as a nation. The formal education system is in the process of fundamental restructuring. New standards are being set and new means of meeting them are being developed.

The opportunity for the BBC to play an enhanced role is also clear. Education and training in the 1990s are increasingly dependent on the use of audio and video technology, but the hardware of modern technology is only as useful as the software that it transmits – the educational programming and support services that the BBC is equipped and ready to supply.

The BBC should grasp this opportunity. It should commit itself to a new strategy to support the education and training of the nation into the 21st century. The key elements of that strategy should be as follows:

■ **Supporting the improvement in the standards of formal education in the U.K.'s schools, colleges and universities by:**

— **Sustaining the BBC's output of programmes for primary schools, secondary schools and the Open University.**

— **Tying schools programming as closely as possible into the National Curricula in England, Wales and Northern Ireland and the curricular guidelines in Scotland.**

— **Applying the very best BBC programme making skills and commissioning the best independent programme makers to provide schools and Open University programmes.**

— **Investing in those educational programming strands (Schools Television and Primary Schools Radio) that consistently reach their audience, and releasing funds from Secondary Schools Radio where it does not reach its audience.**

■ **Improving the nation's vocational skill base, and particularly its language skills, by:**

— **Developing strands of programming to support the pursuit of National Vocational Qualifications (NVQs).**

— **Developing additional strands of language skills programming, supported by a full range of backup products and services.**

— **Building up BBC Select, the BBC's subscription funded overnight downloading service, to provide access for professional and vocational training programmes.**

■ **Adapting and applying modern media technology to enhance the educational process by:**

— **The increased use of the night-time hours for downloading of schools programming and BBC Select services onto video cassette recorders.**

— **The extended use of video and audio cassettes to distribute BBC educational programming in an efficient and cost effective way.**

— **The development of interactive technology to enhance the appeal and impact of the BBC's educational programming.**

In order to ensure the single-minded pursuit of this strategy, the BBC has established a single organisational unit – BBC Education – to coordinate all of its educational activities across all media. It covers Languages, Schools, Open University production and Continuing Education, as well as taking overall responsibility for BBC Select. It will coordinate the various audio, video and publishing products which the BBC needs to develop and distribute in pursuit of its educative role, both in the U.K. and overseas.

In addition, the BBC should extend and enhance the output of 'educative' general programming in the peak time and other schedules. A high proportion of the BBC's general programming makes knowledge available to viewers and listeners in a way that maximises the opportunities for learning. The BBC should maintain and even increase the prominence of this programming. It should place particular priority on:

■ **Science and natural history programming, which covers the natural world with authority and imagination.**

■ **Current affairs, documentary and feature programming, which portrays the contemporary world, and political and social history programming, which explores our heritage.**

■ **Religious, moral and ethical programming, which maintains a prominent place in the radio and television schedules for programmes of religious worship, music and journalism, covering a wide range of faiths, portraying many aspects of religious culture, and exploring the major moral and ethical issues of our time.**

**Mad About Music**
BBC Schools Television

**Etoiles – Multi media initiative**
BBC Education Publishing

**Educative programming**

**Trials of Life**
BBC 1

**Everyman**
BBC 1

■ **Music, drama and arts programming, which broadens the audience's experience and understanding of its cultural heritage and the contemporary arts**

## COMMUNICATING BETWEEN THE U.K. AND ABROAD

The BBC is already one of the primary sources of communication between the U.K. and abroad. Through World Service Radio, World Service Television and the sale and distribution of programmes and other material, the BBC regularly reaches audiences of more than 120 million people around the world. Its many services for international audiences bring credit to the U.K., and enhance the reputation of British culture and democracy.

BBC-made programmes are also the focus of one of the U.K.'s most successful and enduring export industries. Its programmes are sold to 120 countries and translated into more than 50 languages. They generate revenues of more than £70 million for the BBC. All of BBC Enterprises' activities – many of which are focused on overseas markets – make a total contribution of more than £50 million to the production of original programming for the BBC. For instance, over 50 per cent of the direct costs of the BBC's natural history programmes are covered by the reinvestment of revenues generated by programme sales and co-productions.

The BBC is therefore already pursuing its international role with commitment – but more potential exists. The combination of new technology and deregulation which is transforming the British broadcasting environment is having a similar effect on the international airwaves. For the first time, broadcasting is becoming a truly international industry. We are already seeing the emergence of pan-European or even global broadcasting organisations, seeking to transmit news, sport, entertainment and other services to audiences around the world.

The BBC can and should work as a major force within this expanding market. It is a natural outlet for British talent and creative skill. It also has the potential to generate additional revenue as a supplement to the licence fee.

But it will not be easy. New opportunities are attracting new competitors, and the BBC will have to strengthen its commitment to international broadcasting in order to maintain its leadership. Its strategy for international broadcasting should have three main elements:

■ **Support, extend and enhance World Service Radio.** The cornerstone of the U.K.'s international broadcasting presence should continue to be World Service Radio – funded by grant-in-aid from the Foreign and Commonwealth Office, but retaining, as part of the BBC, the independence and objectivity on which its reputation is based. Its services should continue to include:

— **24 hours a day of English-language broadcasting to audiences around the world, supplemented by special programmes of regional interest.**

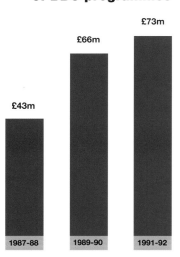

**Growing sales\***
**of BBC programmes**

£73m

£66m

£43m

| 1987-88 | 1989-90 | 1991-92 |

\*Includes co-productions' contribution

Source: BBC Enterprises.

38

## 3

— Over 500 hours a week of broadcasting in 39 languages or more, reaching audiences in excess of 100 million people.

— English teaching by radio and television, including the provision of relevant backup material.

The FCO 'prescription' for the World Service is being relaxed to allow more effective use of resources and more flexibility in responding to broadcasting priorities. Within agreed limits, the World Service will be able to extend its services in response to audience demand, without going through a cumbersome process of official approval. Beyond that, the World Service and the FCO should work together to identify new ways of developing and adapting the service to extend its reach and impact.

■ **Develop World Service Television.** The BBC has already achieved an extraordinary success in the rapid early distribution of World Service Television. Since its launch in 1990, it has established a substantial presence in Asia through its partnership with Star TV, in Africa through its partnership with M-Net and in Canada through its partnership with CBC. In addition, it intends to develop a truly competitive broadcasting business for the BBC in Europe – and has plans in place to launch distinct services of news and entertainment for the European audience. In a world in which television is increasingly the dominant medium of communication, these services are critical to the U.K.'s international broadcasting reputation and impact. The BBC strategy for the expansion of World Service Television should focus on:

— Developing sound financial arrangements, independent of licence fee money, to sustain the various services – building on the precedent that has now been established in commercial partnership arrangements with Star TV, M-Net and CBC.

— The provision of continuous international news services for satellite and cable audiences in overseas markets, seeking to challenge the U.S.-owned Cable News Network International as the primary source of international news.

— Seeking as a high priority to secure distribution in Eastern Europe and in the countries of the former U.S.S.R.

■ **Intensify the BBC's participation in the international market for programme sales and co-productions.** The BBC should continue to develop its leading position in the international market for television programmes and related services. The BBC's strategy for the expansion of its programme sales and co-production activity should focus on:

— Increasing coordination of BBC Enterprises and BBC programme makers to ensure full international exploitation of the BBC's programmes.

— Increasingly inventive use of the BBC's archive in international markets.

— Development of long term co-production partnerships and output deals with overseas broadcasters in key markets.

**Communicating between the U.K. and abroad**

**Mikhail Gorbachev after the coup**
BBC World ServiceTV

**Terry Waite interviewed**
BBC World Service

**Demonstrators in Peking's Tiananmen Square**

# A Single Coherent Broadcasting Organisation 4

— **a single strategy**

— **complementary television channels**

— **adapting radio**

— **regional diversity**

— **a clear commercial framework**

Whave outlined new and refined programming strategies in line with the BBC's public purpose. But what kind of broadcasting organisation is needed to ensure that these programmes are effectively delivered to the audience who want them?

Some have argued that this task could be performed by several different broadcasting organisations, rather than by a single BBC. They have suggested that the BBC could be broken up into a series of smaller units, each of them operating independently. The aim would be to encourage a diversity of approaches and competition for public funding.

**The public is best served by a single coherent broadcasting organisation**

But we believe that the public is best served by a single, coherent broadcasting organisation dedicated to delivering programmes of quality and distinction across all media. The benefits of a single BBC are substantial:

- A single, coherent role and strategy for publicly funded broadcasting in Britain.

- Concentrated investment in specialist skills and expertise at a level which could not be duplicated by a number of smaller organisations.

- The extended use of that specialist expertise across all of the BBC's radio and television channels to deliver the best possible programming to each audience.

- Complementary scheduling of programmes across radio and television to ensure maximum choice for viewers and listeners, particularly at peak hours.

- A coherent range of radio, television and other programme services for people overseas.

The importance of these benefits is increasingly reflected in the way the BBC works. It takes a strategic approach – assessing the needs of the audience in each area – and structures its organisation to meet these needs in the most effective way. The highest priority is therefore given to deploying staff and resources to the service of the public as follows:

- News and Current Affairs journalists serve both television and radio, as part of a single 'bi-media' directorate.

- Similarly, the BBC's regional journalists and production staff operate across both media.

- The BBC's previously dispersed educational activities have now been restructured into a single directorate serving television, radio and other support media.

- Religious programmes are being brought together in one centre.

- The World Service now reaches its huge international audience through both radio and television.

- Comedy and light entertainment programmes and talent developed on radio are often transferred to television and vice versa.

## 4

■ **BBC sports coverage is aimed at ensuring universal access to major events by the use of both media.**

■ **Live music such as the BBC Proms, major artistic performances, and political and ceremonial occasions are frequently the subject of shared and complementary coverage by BBC radio and television.**

■ **BBC staff are increasingly being trained in multiple skills to make possible working in different media, with improved career opportunities and increased productivity.**

The benefits of this coherent approach are delivered to audiences through the BBC's different services. These services must be scheduled and organised in a complementary manner to extend choice for viewers and listeners and to deliver programmes at the appropriate time and in the appropriate medium. But they must also have individual identities and priorities.

## PRIORITIES FOR NETWORK TELEVISION

Two complementary television channels are the only way of ensuring sufficient airtime – particularly during peak viewing periods – for the full array of public service programmes outlined in Chapter 3. They are also the only means of ensuring that those programmes are scheduled to extend choice both for a wide audience and for different groups within that audience.

The priorities for Network Television are therefore to develop and maintain distinctive and focused programming and scheduling strategies for BBC 1 and BBC 2.

■ **BBC 1 should be the main national channel, delivering quality programmes to a wide audience.** It should:

— **Ensure that high quality news and current affairs programmes are offered to viewers at the most accessible times.**

— **Schedule an increasing proportion of new drama and comedy series.**

— **Develop new and fresh light entertainment formats.**

— **Schedule major documentaries about British life, history and culture in prime time.**

— **Offer high quality children's programmes, including drama, entertainment and information.**

— **Ensure that religious programmes retain a prominent place in the schedule.**

— **Schedule quality, accessible arts, science and natural history programmes in prime time.**

— **Join with BBC 2 in ensuring that the major political, ceremonial and sporting events which are of importance to the nation are made universally available, and covered in depth with a sense of occasion.**

# A Single Coherent Broadcasting Organisation

■   **BBC 2 should be the more innovative, experimental channel, addressing different groups within the audience.**  It should challenge and surprise its audiences, and set out to change the public perception of what television can do.  In particular, BBC 2 should:

— Inform the national debate by ensuring that a wide range of important issues is reported, debated and analysed in depth.

— Commission new writers, composers, performers and programme makers, calling on these new talents to generate much of BBC 2's drama, comedy, music and cultural programming.

— Schedule innovative and risk taking programmes in prime time.

— Broadcast arts programmes which take a fresh, new approach as well as an authoritative view.  It should develop relationships with national institutions in the arts to ensure quality coverage of artistic life in the U.K.

— Ensure that programmes for special interest groups (whether religious, ethnic or community of interest) are offered when these groups are available to watch.

— Play a major role in creating opportunities for education by scheduling a wide range of formal and informal educational programming.

■   **BBC 1 and BBC 2 should work together to provide complementary services which capture the additional benefits to the audience of having two BBC channels, broadcasting in parallel:**

— Within their distinctive identities, BBC 1 and BBC 2 should apply complementary scheduling and commissioning strategies to ensure that the widest range of quality programmes are made available to U.K. audiences at accessible times.

— They should work together to give full reflection to regional and cultural diversity in the BBC's programmes.

— They should ensure that the BBC plays its full educative role, including the provision of formal educational programmes for schools and the Open University.

— They should encourage the development and 'cross-fertilisation' between the two channels of new talent, new formats and higher risk programmes.

## PRIORITIES FOR RADIO

The BBC's pursuit of its public purpose will also have profound implications for the BBC's radio services.  Their nature and character will change markedly between now and the end of the next Charter period.

That is not unusual.  Radio is a highly dynamic medium, constantly changing and adapting to meet listeners' needs.  The existing radio services were themselves born out of the need to change and adapt to the environment of 20 years ago.  Since the beginning of the current Charter in 1981, there have been substantial evolutionary changes in the format, schedule, presentation style and target audiences of Radios 1, 2, 3 and 4 – as well as the introduction of a new service, Radio 5. The BBC is therefore well used to adapting its radio services in order to respond to a changing market.

Given the fluid and dynamic nature of the radio marketplace, it is impossible to define precisely the radio services that will run through the next Charter period. The number and range of services will depend on the overall funding available. It is, however, important to establish as precisely as possible the priorities that should govern the development and adaptation of the BBC's radio services over that time, and we believe that they should be:

■ **To assign priority to those networks and services which are truly distinctive and unlikely ever to be matched in the commercial marketplace.** While each of the BBC's existing radio networks have distinctive elements to them, Radios 3 and 4 currently come closest to being unique. Radio 4's high quality speech output consisting of news and current affairs, a wide range of drama, comedy, documentaries, magazine programmes and special interest programmes is unmatched in the world. Radio 3's commitment to cultural patronage and excellence across a wide range of music and performers is unlikely to be duplicated by commercial stations. But there is room for improvement: Radio 4 should be able to speak to a wider range of audience groups and Radio 3 should be more accessible and appealing to classical music listeners. However, both have marked out a highly valued place in the broadcasting market which should be sustained in the long term.

■ **To create and establish a continuous news service.** As we outlined earlier, the BBC can only fulfil its most critical role as the platform for national debate if it develops continuous news services on television and radio. The BBC is uniquely equipped to create such a service on radio – it can deploy its existing bi-media newsgathering capability, draw upon the World Service, and benefit from the experience of running News FM during the Gulf War. Such a service has been announced and will be a major priority for the BBC.

■ **To ensure that the BBC's other radio audiences are offered recognisably distinctive services by the BBC.** During an era of limited competition, the BBC has rendered an important public service by delivering services consisting mostly of pop and popular music. Those services have always been given added distinction by their authoritative news coverage, original programming, social action initiatives and live performance coverage. However, these are no longer times of limited competition, but rather of a proliferation of commercial radio services, most of them providing pop and popular music programmes. In these circumstances, the BBC now needs to develop recognisably distinctive and innovative services for those audiences for whom radio is the most important and influential broadcasting medium. The principal characteristics of those services should be:

**Radio is a highly dynamic medium, constantly changing and adapting to meet listeners' needs**

— Pop and popular music programming which puts the emphasis on range, diversity and innovation, and which provides in-depth coverage of music for particular listening interests.

— An emphasis on live performance, new work and ideas.

— A higher degree of speech content than commercial music stations, with news and information, humour, drama and social action.

— A presentation style which is clearly informative and intelligent.

■ **To serve the audiences for education and sports radio.** The BBC should be committed to serving the audiences who look to radio for educational support – both at the primary school level and in Continuing Education – and for authoritative sports coverage. Most recently those audiences have been served primarily on Radio 5, which has been newly created at very low cost to provide extended service to BBC listeners. As the BBC modifies and adapts its portfolio of radio networks over time, it should ensure that the audiences for education and sports radio are well served.

■ **To make a major continuing commitment to British culture and the arts.** As part of its role in 'expressing British culture and entertainment', it is important for the BBC, on radio as on television, to play an active role in cultural development. It should nurture, originate and commission new work, and provide long term support to major cultural institutions and events. The most prominent of these are the BBC orchestras. They form an integral part of the BBC's function as a cultural patron, supporting live performance and originating the widest possible repertory of music, including new commissions. They also fulfil a vital regional, national and international role in our musical life. Their role and funding should now be considered individually. The BBC should reassert its commitment to the symphony orchestras on the grounds of editorial needs, while discussing ways in which they can play a full part in the national pattern of orchestral funding and provision.

Over the next few years, and into the next Charter period, the BBC should adapt and where necessary reshape its radio services to deliver these priorities, and to respond to the public debate which is about to take place.

## PRIORITIES FOR REGIONAL BROADCASTING

If the BBC is to inform the national debate, express British culture and entertainment, and educate its audience, it must have a programme making and broadcasting presence across the regions of the U.K.

In reaching this view, we have considered the arguments of those who question whether the BBC should be a regional broadcaster. They point to the continuing federal structure of ITV with its binding requirement to be a regional broadcaster, to the local and regional presence of Independent Local Radio, and to the strain on BBC resources of meeting the local and regional broadcasting requirement on both

**The BBC is the British Broadcasting Corporation, not the London Broadcasting Corporation**

television and radio. They ask whether the BBC can afford to be a regional broadcaster.

We believe that the BBC must be a regional broadcaster if it is fully to deliver its public service purpose. The BBC is the **British** Broadcasting Corporation, not the **London** Broadcasting Corporation. It should remain in touch with the views and priorities of its audience throughout the U.K.; it should have a journalistic presence in all parts of the country; it should draw its programmes from centres of excellence in the nations and regions of the U.K.; and it should reflect in its programmes the regional and cultural diversity which so enriches Britain. The BBC is uniquely placed in the broadcasting industry to act as a major influence in bringing together these different elements for a national audience.

It is true that the structure of both ITV and commercial radio goes some way to reflect this regional identity and that plans for Channel 5 include ideas for a new kind of 'city television'. But Channel 5 will not cover the whole population and the extension of choice in regional television will be less than that in national television. Channel 4 seems likely to remain an essentially national service and satellite broadcasters are neither technically equipped nor economically disposed to offer regional or local coverage. On radio, ILR is increasingly focused on segments of the pop and popular music market, with less and less emphasis on local news, information and discussion.

The BBC's regional broadcasting priorities should therefore be:

■ **To commission and make network programmes right across the U.K.** The BBC should make network radio and television programmes in designated regional production centres – in Belfast, Birmingham, Bristol, Cardiff, Glasgow and Manchester – as well as London. A substantial proportion of its network television and radio production expenditure should be invested outside the South East, and it should encourage the further development of an independent production sector outside the South East. As part of this commitment, the BBC has already established centres of programming excellence around the U.K. which will specialise in different genres. These include Natural History and Features programming in Bristol; Religion, Sport and Youth and Entertainment features in Manchester; and Drama, Multicultural and Leisure programming in Birmingham. These policies will ensure that the BBC reflects and encourages the creative, production and craft skills of people throughout the U.K.

■ **To deliver an authoritative local and regional news and current affairs service on television and radio.** There is a multitude of issues that are high on the regional agenda, and have a direct and far-reaching effect on people's lives. Many of the major national policies raise different issues in different parts of the country, are subject to different solutions and are implemented in different ways, as the result of intense local and regional debate. Then there are more intrinsically local and regional issues – political, social, religious, industrial and commercial. The BBC needs to report, analyse and debate these issues fully for local audiences. It should:

**Regional broadcasting**

**The Archers, made in Birmingham**
Radio 4

**Rab C Nesbit, made in Scotland**
BBC 2

**The Old Devils, made in Wales**
BBC 2

**Close Up North**
BBC North

**Jim Dougal at Stormont**
BBC Northern Ireland

— Deliver a daily regional television news service, supported by weekly current affairs and parliamentary programmes across the year.

— Continue to focus English local radio services on speech and information – to complement music based ILR services. BBC local radio should be all speech at key times when the largest audiences are available to listen; match the standards for all BBC journalism 7 days a week; be a focal point for community debate and action; recognise the different religious and ethnic populations; and give the country's multiracial and multilingual groups a radio voice in the community. An example of this approach is the highly successful 'Asian Network' broadcast on the BBC's local radio stations in the Midlands.

■ **To invest in a high level of information, cultural and entertainment programme provision for Scotland, Wales and Northern Ireland.** We believe that as a national broadcaster in these three countries, the BBC should provide audiences with a range of broadly based, but clearly defined, programme services which acknowledge and celebrate their differences. The exact nature of those dedicated programme services should be determined by what it is that makes those countries different – including politics, education, the arts, entertainment, sport, comedy and religion. The BBC should be a cultural patron in each of these countries – involved in their respective communities, supporting their writers, artists and orchestras. And it should play an active role in nurturing and promoting the languages that have such a special place in the lives and traditions of Scotland and Wales, including the production of high quality Welsh language programmes for S4C.

PRIORITIES FOR SECONDARY DISTRIBUTION

Finally, the BBC should play an increasingly active role in secondary markets as an important dimension of its public purpose, and in order to generate additional funds for reinvestment in core programming services.

There are powerful reasons for doing so. There is considerable demand for BBC programmes in the international broadcasting market, and many opportunities for the BBC to work with overseas producers on co-production ventures. There is also increasing demand from consumers in the U.K. for videos, audio tapes, books and magazines which add significantly to their understanding and appreciation of BBC programmes. And people are keen to invest in satellite delivered broadcasting services which provide secondary outlets for programming originally developed by the BBC.

Profits from the BBC's involvement in these markets are re-invested to enable it to produce more original programming for licence payers.

There should be two main priorities for the BBC in secondary markets:

■ **To continue to develop the BBC's participation in secondary markets within a clearly defined commercial framework.** The BBC should continue to develop these services, several of which have substantial potential for expansion. It should do so within a very clear commercial framework which applies a number of strict criteria to the services offered by BBC Enterprises. In particular, those services must:

— **Spring from the BBC's core commitment to meet the programme needs of its audience.**

— **Observe fair trading practices.**

— **Not draw on licence revenue, but rather earn a positive financial return for the licence payer.**

■ **To take part in the development of the commercially funded market for specialist channels on satellite and cable.** Subscription television is set to be the fastest growing sector of the broadcasting market through the 1990s and beyond as new satellite and cable services rapidly gain household penetration and share. It is entirely consistent with the BBC's public service role and objectives for it to support or supply programming to satellite channels, which supplement and deliver greater depth than is possible on the core licence fee funded services. These might include:

— **A continuous news channel, of the kind we described earlier in this chapter.**

— **Channels which use the BBC's archives; for example, the collaborative venture with Thames Television to launch U.K. Gold on the Astra satellite.**

The BBC should work with partners to develop these and other options which offer extended choice to potential subscribers. This will build on the experience the BBC already has in supplying programmes to, and collaborating with, specialist cable and satellite services.

● ● ●

In summary, Chapters 3 and 4 have outlined a body of ideas about the future evolution of the BBC's programme strategies and broadcasting services within a single broadcasting organisation. These ideas reflect the BBC's track record and traditions. But they also reflect the new broadcasting environment and the need for the BBC to pursue a clear public purpose within it. The BBC that emerges from this period of change should have an even clearer and more valued place in the range of choices available to viewers and listeners.

# Delivering Value for Money

5

— improved efficiency

— radical reorganisation

— reduced overheads

— more money for programmes

I n the new broadcasting environment the BBC should do more than change and adapt its services. It should also change the way in which it develops and delivers those services. It should aim to meet the highest achievable standards of efficiency and cost effectiveness – and thus to deliver outstanding value for money.

The pursuit of this objective is a central element of the BBC's public purpose. The public that funds the BBC justifiably expects as much of its money as possible to be spent on programmes. This means that as little as possible of it should go into overheads, and that spending on unnecessary bureaucracy, unproductive resources and under-used capacity should be eliminated.

The standards of efficiency and cost effectiveness set by the broadcasting industry have not always been very challenging. For much of its history, the BBC has been part of a high cost industry. ITV and ILR as well as the BBC were characterised by entrenched working practices, cumbersome organisation structures, over-staffing and poor industrial relations.

But all that has changed. The broadcasting industry as a whole has started to move towards a new 'structural model'. Under competitive and economic pressure, both ITV and ILR have made substantial reductions in their staffing levels and costs. And in order to do this, they have made radical changes in the way in which they work.

**The BBC is determined to meet the highest industry standards and provide outstanding value for money**

The BBC is determined to meet the highest industry standards and provide value for money. It has changed the way it works. It has become smaller and reduced its costs. It is adjusting its internal structure and working practices more accurately to reflect its public purposes. Examples of the latest initiatives include:

■ Reducing its domestic television and radio staff by approximately 7,000 between 1986 and the end of 1993, while creating 1,000 new jobs in areas of enhanced or extended service like the broadcasting of Parliament, regional journalism and arts programmes on television.

■ Continuing to reduce its property portfolio. The strategy which began in 1986 will mean the BBC giving up 23 London buildings, a 12.5 per cent reduction in occupied space, and a 70 per cent reduction in rental paid by the end of 1995.

■ Reducing its number of television studios and stages from 27 to 14 by the end of 1992, and closing 17 radio studios.

■ Reducing its number of network television outside broadcast units from 23 to 14 by the end of 1992, and reducing the radio outside broadcast fleet by 20.

■ Improving the efficiency and effectiveness of the World Service through the policies which were recently endorsed by the National Audit Office.

All of these initiatives have released more money for programme making, increased the BBC's efficiency, and eliminated underused plant and resources. And even more change in the BBC's structure and working practices is now being introduced.

## PRODUCER CHOICE

At the heart of the process of change is the **Producer Choice** initiative, which is currently being implemented throughout the BBC. Producer Choice has profound implications for the organisational, financial and operational characteristics of the BBC. This is how Producer Choice will work:

■ Those who commission programmes for broadcasting will draw up strategies in line with the BBC's public purposes. Funds will be allocated to them on the basis of these strategies.

■ Programmes will then be commissioned either from BBC departments or from independent programme makers.

■ BBC producers will be free to choose whether to buy their resources (studios, camera crews, design, scenery, graphics, etc.) from inhouse resource departments or from the external market.

■ The BBC's resource departments will need to earn their funding by attracting programme making business in competition with the growing outside facilities market.

■ BBC programme makers will have formal contractual relationships with resource suppliers – whether inhouse or external – buying specified services at an agreed price. In their turn, BBC programme makers will have contractual relationships with the Channel Controllers who commission and schedule their programmes.

The results of Producer Choice will be as follows:

■ Funding will be related to programme strategies and based on best industry practice.

■ The BBC's competitiveness in both programme making and resource provision will be tested against the outside market.

■ The BBC will only retain those resources for which there is a demand from programme makers.

■ There will be lower overheads.

■ More funds will be released for programme making.

■ Decision making will be devolved to those responsible for the BBC's core activity of programme making.

■ The BBC will become financially more transparent and therefore more accountable.

As part of this strategy, the BBC will operate on a flexible and open basis with the independent programme making sector. It will commit itself to commissioning the best programming ideas whether they are offered internally or by independents. As a result, in some genres, the 25 per cent television quota will be exceeded and in some it will not. It will be treated as a floor requirement overall. In radio, clear targets for independent production have been set by the BBC and will be met as the independent sector of the radio production industry develops.

**Producer Choice has profound implications for the organisation of the BBC**

OTHER INITIATIVES

The BBC is also taking a number of other initiatives in preparation for the introduction of Producer Choice:

**The BBC is taking a tough-minded approach to streamlining its overheads at all levels**

■ **Streamlined resources and overheads.** The BBC is taking a tough-minded approach to streamlining its overheads at all levels. Costs are being cut substantially and in future support services will be managed with rigorous internal discipline.

There are five key elements to this programme of resources and overhead savings:

— **Overheads.** The BBC has recently conducted a fundamental review of its overhead structure to ensure that its costs are as low as possible and that budget holders are able to determine service levels and suppliers. It is redefining and reducing the role of the Centre, focusing it on a small number of essential tasks. It is also applying this same focused approach to the overhead structures of its Directorates.

— **Property.** The BBC is also reviewing its property portfolio which carries with it substantial direct and indirect costs. Through the policy of charging for property costs, the BBC expects to accelerate its programme of rationalisation.

— **Resources.** The BBC is continuing the process of removing plant and resources capacity which will be unnecessary and under-used when 25 per cent of its television programmes are made by the independent sector. In recent years, it has withdrawn a significant number of under-used studios and Outside Broadcast units.

— **Direct costs.** The BBC is planning for direct cost savings and productivity improvements as the resource departments put together their business plans.

— **Provision of services.** The BBC should contract out all service activities which can be provided more efficiently and/or effectively in the outside market. This process has already begun with substantial benefits to the BBC's efficiency and/or quality of internal services. The objective should be for the BBC to have only the internal resources that it absolutely needs to serve its key programme making and broadcasting activities.

■ **Technical research**. The BBC will adopt a similar approach to its technical research operations. It will maintain high calibre technical research capabilities but, like all other resources, they will be subject to evaluation against the external market. In the past, the BBC's technical research capabilities have enabled it to take a leading role in the development of modern broadcasting technology, with enormous benefit to licence payers.

The overriding goals of technical research within the BBC are, and should remain:

— To extend the audience accessibility and attractiveness of all its broadcasting services.

— To help reduce the costs of programme making and transmission.

## 5

■  **Transmission**.  BBC Transmission provides transmission facilities for BBC radio and television.  It also generates income, within guidelines agreed with the Home Secretary, by development of sites, project management and consultancy.  Future arrangements for transmission must ensure that the BBC can guarantee:

—  Cost effective services for the viewer and listener, with a practical balance drawn between technical quality and cost in the interests of all licence payers.

—  The flexibility to respond rapidly to the changing needs of the audience through modified investment plans.

—  The avoidance of any elements of monopoly which could drive costs up and standards down.

—  Continual testing of new technologies, such as high definition/widescreen television, digital television transmission, digital audio broadcasting and satellite delivery for both radio and television to assess their ability to deliver real benefits at reasonable cost to all viewers and listeners.

—  The security and availability of transmission facilities for World Service programmes.

■  **Employment and training.**  The BBC will pursue a rigorous programme of change to create a working environment that attracts and fosters the very best talent, and thus generates excellent programmes.  It will:

—  Ensure that its staff are offered the best training available.  Throughout the BBC, people are being trained in multiple skills so that they can be deployed as effectively as possible. This is enabling the use of smaller crews in television programme production and news and current affairs, as well as the introduction of jobs that combine programme production and studio operation in network radio.

—  Reduce the number of layers of management structure and empower individuals and teams to manage without excessive supervision, control and bureaucracy.

—  Build on its existing equal opportunities and fair recruitment policies to ensure that it meets best employment practice.

—  Reward staff appropriately for the contribution they make towards achieving the BBC's goals.

—  Ensure that it meets high standards of care for protecting the health and safety of its staff .

• • •

The BBC of the future will deliver clear public purposes which are different from those of the commercial broadcasting market.  But it will use the market to help achieve its purposes and to test its efficiency.  The initiatives outlined in this chapter will enable the BBC to liberate resources from unproductive use and put the highest possible proportion of its income directly into making high quality programmes at the lowest achievable cost. The BBC will thus deliver outstanding value for money to the licence payer.

**A working environment that attracts and fosters the very best talent**

# Harnessing Technology

6

— high quality broadcasting

— cost effective delivery

**1987**

Joint award for teleswitching

**1992**

Nicam Digital Stereo

**BBC Engineering - granted the Queen's Award for Technological Achievement five times**

BBC high definition television sports coverage

T he history of broadcasting has been characterised by extraordinary advances in technology. Each of these advances has expanded the range and enhanced the quality of broadcasting services to the viewer and listener. Over the last decade, the pace of technological change has accelerated. Since the BBC's current Charter period began in 1981, we have seen the emergence of direct to home satellite broadcasting, of cable television and of the video cassette recorder as a mass market product. These technological advances are so significant as to transform broadcasting supply and demand.

The BBC has often made important contributions to the development of broadcasting technology. BBC engineers have played major roles in the progressive enhancement of sound and picture quality on television, in the development and expansion of FM stereo services on radio and in the creation of teletext services. More recently, they have been involved in the development of NICAM digital stereo sound on television.

The BBC's policy has always been to harness technology to the service of the public. The licence payer would not have been well served had the BBC remained a purely radio broadcaster, unable to influence the quality of the emerging television medium; or if it had stuck resolutely to black and white television, when colour technology became available. No more would it now be appropriate for the BBC to limit itself to old technologies, which may or may not eventually become as obsolete as valve radio and black and white television.

■ The process of technological change in broadcasting is by no means complete. At least three major initiatives are under way, each of which could dramatically increase the number and enhance the quality of broadcasting services:

— **High definition/widescreen television.** Broadcasters may soon be able to offer improved quality pictures, employing either high definition or widescreen television technology. BBC engineers have played an active role in the development of HDTV systems. Many HDTV programmes have been produced by the BBC, including coverage of tennis from Wimbledon, the FA Cup Final, Mahler's Eighth Symphony and the drama series, 'The Ginger Tree'. Widescreen TV, which is especially beneficial to films and sport, is seen as a possible interim development prior to the introduction of HDTV in the longer term.

— **Digital television.** Parallel work is going on to develop the capability for digital compression of television signals. Digital transmission could dramatically increase the number and quality of services available to viewers. For instance, the spectrum currently used to provide the four existing terrestrial television services might also be able to accommodate four digital HDTV services or many more digital TV services of a quality comparable with the existing services. Similar techniques could also be used to squeeze more services within each satellite TV channel.

— **Digital audio broadcasting.** The application of digital compression to audio signals offers an equal, if not greater, potential for improvement in delivery of radio services to listeners. It offers the possibility of much more efficient use of the radio spectrum, with five or six stereo FM services occupying the space currently taken by one. It would also improve the convenience and reliability of radio reception for listeners using portable and car radios, as well as offering CD quality reception for listeners using hi-fi equipment. Digital audio broadcasting delivered by satellite direct to the listener also opens up new opportunities for the BBC in its international broadcasting role.

As always, however, there is a high degree of uncertainty surrounding the likely pace of technological change. How quickly will new technologies be ready for market introduction? How rapidly will they be taken up in the marketplace? What impact will they have on the broadcasting environment? These are questions which can often only be answered with a well-educated guess.

For this reason, the ideas for the BBC's future role contained in this document primarily reflect the current state of broadcasting technology, and anticipate the way in which the broadcasting environment will respond to proven technological advance.

Nevertheless, the BBC's thinking about the future is highly sensitive to the potential impact of technologies that are not yet fully developed, and certainly not proven.

The BBC's future approach to technology should continue to be driven by the objective of providing high quality, cost effective programmes and services to viewers and listeners. It should not view itself as primarily a research organisation or a technological pioneer. But, like NHK in Japan, it should be prepared to play a leadership role in the advance of broadcasting technology to the service of the public. It will therefore have the following priorities:

**Providing high quality, cost effective services to viewers and listeners**

■ To deliver its core services to viewers and listeners using known technology.

■ Not to discontinue existing transmission arrangements until new technology is widely in use.

■ To play its leadership role, either by offering new services or by simultaneously transmitting existing services on both old and new technology.

■ Therefore, in the short term, to create services that apply existing satellite and cable technology.

■ In the longer term, to provide selective support to the development of widescreen/ high definition television, digital television and digital audio broadcasting.

● ● ●

In this way, the BBC can ensure that its services to the licence payer and to the international audience are always the product of the most modern and effective technology.

## Appropriate Funding

7

— options reviewed

— licence fee meets public purposes

— supplements from secondary services

W e have considered a wide range of options for the future funding of the BBC – including advertising, sponsorship, subscription and direct grant funding of all or some of the BBC's core services. Our analysis of these options has led us to the view that the BBC's core services should continue to be funded primarily by the licence fee. However, we also believe that the licence fee should be supplemented by other sources of revenue – notably subscription fees – from secondary distribution activities.

This chapter assesses each funding option against the roles and objectives for the BBC outlined in Chapter 2 and the proposed evolution of its services in Chapters 3 and 4.

ADVERTISING FUNDING?

We have considered the option that the BBC's core services should be wholly or partially funded by advertising revenue. The case for that option rests on the following contentions:

- Licence fee funding is anomalous in a modern broadcasting environment characterised by competition and choice.

- In such an environment, advertising is the most commonly used, tried and tested mechanism for the funding of broadcasters.

- The BBC's principal competitors – ITV, Channel 4, INR and ILR – are required to secure their revenue from advertising, and licence fee funding gives the BBC an unfair competitive advantage over them.

- Increased competition for advertising revenue would drive down the price of advertising, help to stimulate the economy, and at the same time impose appropriate financial disciplines on the BBC and ITV.

- The experience of ITV and Channel 4 under tight regulation suggests that advertising funded broadcasters, appropriately regulated and controlled, can meet many of the roles and objectives of public service broadcasting.

- Even if not appropriate as the sole source of BBC funding, advertising would be appropriate as part of a mixed funding base, and by limiting the amount and positioning of advertising time or by focusing advertising on particular services (e.g., on Radio 1), it could be kept relatively unobtrusive.

However, we believe that these contentions do not stand up to scrutiny, and that advertising on the BBC's core services is undesirable for the following reasons:

**Advertising primarily rewards ratings and share**

- The first priority of any advertising funded broadcaster is quite properly to maximise profits in order to sustain the business and generate a return to shareholders. It is not to pursue single-mindedly the public service roles and objectives outlined in Chapter 2. Advertising primarily rewards ratings and share rather than the intensity of audience interest in and appreciation of the programming. As a consequence, advertising-funded broadcasters tend only to schedule programmes with large audience appeal in prime time.

- Research shows that there is widespread public support for the continued existence of advertising-free services. That support is particularly for those services which appeal to young people and children, in contrast to the large and increasing number of advertising led commercial services that are strongly targeted at those groups.

- There is a growing body of evidence that there will not be enough advertising revenue to go round. Although advertising grew rapidly in the 1980s, it has stagnated through the recession and is expected to grow much less rapidly in the 1990s. Whatever growth there is will be needed to fund the newly independent Channel 4 and the newly created Channel 5 on terrestrial television, the new satellite and cable television networks, and INR and ILR on radio. The introduction of advertising on the BBC would not appreciably increase the size of the advertising pool, and would simply precipitate an intensified battle for revenue with stark consequences for programming.

- If the BBC were to take advertising, the strength of its programme making and broadcasting reputation would ensure that it garnered a significant share of the available advertising revenue. This would certainly limit the funds available to all other commercial broadcasters, and thus reduce the overall level of quality, competition and choice in the broadcasting market.

- Several overseas public service broadcasters are required by their governments to be partially funded by advertising. Their experience demonstrates that it is difficult both to meet distinctive public service goals and to be a strong and sustainable commercial player at the same time. For instance, deregulation in France and Germany has resulted in a significant reduction in public service broadcasters' audience share, making it increasingly difficult for them to raise the necessary advertising revenue to fund the production of distinctive, high quality programming. And in Canada, the need for CBC to schedule output that competes with U.S. overspill media for audience and advertising revenues has undermined its distinctive programming proposition.

We therefore believe that there should be no advertising on the BBC's core services, since any step in that direction would compromise the public purpose of the BBC and would dilute the revenue available for quality commercial services.

SPONSORSHIP FUNDING?

The second option that we have considered is that some or all of the BBC's programmes and/or services should be funded by sponsorship. The case for this option rests on the following arguments:

- Sponsorship is a proven form of broadcasting funding in other countries and is starting to emerge as a potential source of funding in the U.K.

- In other countries, and increasingly in the U.K., sponsorship is sometimes a supplementary source of funds for large scale, high quality and necessarily high cost programming – particularly major sporting events (e.g., the Rugby World Cup) and occasionally drama series (e.g., Inspector Morse).

**There should be no advertising on the BBC's core services**

■ Since most of the major sporting events and an increasing number of the most important cultural events that the BBC covers are commercially sponsored, it is reasonable to consider whether the broadcast coverage of those events should also be commercially sponsored.

We do believe that BBC coverage of sponsored sporting and artistic events, organised by outside bodies, is firmly in the public interest. Sponsorship is often an appropriate and attractive source of funding for such events. It can be the critical factor in extending the number and range of events that are staged. The BBC should develop partnerships with sponsors to bring public events to the screen and to the airwaves.

We do not, however, believe that BBC programmes should be sponsored for the following reasons:

■ Sponsorship is a particular form of advertising. As such, its effect is to intensify the pressures on broadcasters to maximise their audience ratings and share. Programmes are only sponsored if they can be expected to attract commercially attractive audiences, so sponsorship can have a marked effect on the kinds of programmes that are made and broadcast.

**Sponsorship is a particular form of advertising**

■ Sponsorship carries with it a high degree of dependence on a limited number of corporate and other sponsors.

■ Sponsorship is unlikely to become anything more than a supplementary source of revenue even for commercially funded programme makers and broadcasters. It is still confined to a relatively small number of programmes for which it provides some but not all of the necessary funds.

■ If the BBC were able to secure sponsorship revenue for programmes, it would most probably be at the expense of existing sporting and artistic events.

SUBSCRIPTION FUNDING?

The third major option for the BBC's funding is subscription. We have assessed the case for allowing all or some of the BBC's core services to be funded directly by subscription payments – a case which rests primarily on the following arguments:

■ Direct payment of subscription fees is a proven mechanism for the funding of broadcasting services in overseas markets, and is becoming an ever more substantial source of revenue in this country.

■ As a voluntary payment mechanism, it is more appropriate to a broadcasting environment of competition and choice than a mandatory licence fee.

■ The technology and infrastructure to enable and support large scale subscription funding of broadcasting already exists or could be quickly developed.

■ Rapid early take-up of subscription funded satellite and cable channels has demonstrated the willingness of consumers to pay voluntarily for broadcasting services – often at levels substantially above the current licence fee. Consumer research has indicated that a high proportion are also willing to pay voluntarily for some or all of the BBC's services, again at levels above the current licence fee.

However, while subscription fees are an increasingly attractive means of funding some broadcasting services, we do not believe that they are an appropriate mechanism for funding the BBC's core services. Our reasons are as follows:

- Whilst subscription is proven as a means of funding movie channels and packages of specialist services, it is not proven as a means of funding channels with mixed schedules of the kind that the BBC needs to provide to fulfil its public purpose. Many believe that this kind of service is unlikely to attract long term subscription funding.

- Moreover, subscription funding of the BBC would divert money away from those new broadcasters who rely on it and would thus reduce choice.

- Subscription would force the BBC to give primacy to commercial considerations rather than public service roles and objectives in designing its services, and particularly to give prominence to programming with high 'box office' appeal, which subscription-funded broadcasters use to attract new subscribers.

- Although scrambling and descrambling technology has now reached the point at which it can be used for terrestrial broadcasting, the cost of making it available to the mass market would be very considerable, and the whole process of switching over to subscription funding would cause enormous disruption to the audience and broadcasting market in general. Independent studies have calculated that if all the households which currently receive BBC television were to move to subscription, consumers would face a bill of nearly £3 billion for decoding equipment.

- Subscription funding of radio services is not now technologically feasible – and does not therefore represent an alternative option to the licence fee.

- Finally, subscription funding would remove the principle of universal access to distinctive, high quality programming services, which we believe to be critical to the BBC's role and objectives as a publicly funded broadcaster.

**Subscription would force the BBC to give primacy to commercial considerations**

As outlined in Chapter 4, we believe that the BBC should participate in the development of a subscription television market – but it should do so to enable the creation of new specialist services, primarily on satellite. We believe that this is the best means of applying subscription as a new source of funding to extend choice and competition in the marketplace. We do not believe that it is the best way of funding the core services of the BBC.

WHAT FORM OF PUBLIC FUNDING?

After reviewing all the available options, we therefore believe that public funding is essential to enable the BBC to sustain universal access to broadcasting services that might not otherwise be adequately funded through commercial sources. We have also explored the question of exactly what form of public funding should be applied to the BBC. In particular, we have considered the option that the BBC's core services should be funded by direct grant from government as an element in the annual programme of public expenditure. The argument for this option is founded on the following perspectives:

- If the BBC were to be funded by direct government grant, drawing upon personal taxation rather than a licence fee, the contribution from individual households would directly reflect their ability to pay.

- In addition, absorption of BBC funding into the general taxation system would substantially reduce the cost of collection and of nonpayment associated with the licence fee, and would thus release significant additional funds for programming.

- The BBC would be much more clearly accountable to Parliament for performance against its public service roles and objectives.

However, we believe very strongly that the BBC's domestic services should not be funded by direct grant from government because:

- The BBC's acknowledged strength as an independent information provider, and particularly as a platform for the national debate, should not be compromised by close association with or dependence on the government of the day. The World Service's editorial independence, despite receiving a direct grant-in-aid, is guaranteed by its existence within an independently funded and chartered body.

- While the costs of collection and nonpayment of the licence fee have in the past been substantial, they are being significantly reduced as a consequence of the initiatives that the BBC has taken since it was given direct control of licence fee collection.

LICENCE FEE FUNDING?

Having considered all of the alternative options, we therefore believe that the licence fee will remain the most appropriate way of funding the BBC's core services. The licence fee is the only available funding mechanism which meets all the criteria for the roles and objectives of those services, and in particular:

- The ability to pursue public service objectives as the highest priorities in programme making and scheduling.

- Freedom from the commercial pressures to maximise audience ratings and share – if necessary at the expense of other objectives.

- Independence from direct government or party political influence.

We believe that there should be a long term commitment to continued licence fee funding of the BBC's core services. If that commitment is to be made, then licence fee revenues should clearly be sufficient to cover the costs of the core services, allowing a broad range of high quality programming on both television and radio. The licence fee should grow at a predictable rate which allows those costs to remain covered.

At current levels, the licence fee represents a daily payment of 22p per household, or a weekly payment of £1.54. By any standards, this is exceptional value for money given that the average household consumes more than 36 hours per week of

**The licence fee will remain the most appropriate way of funding the BBC's core services**

**Comparative daily cost of colour TV licence fee**

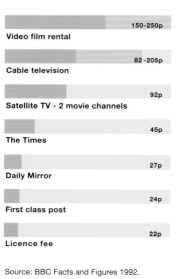

| | |
|---|---|
| Video film rental | 150-250p |
| Cable television | 82-205p |
| Satellite TV - 2 movie channels | 92p |
| The Times | 45p |
| Daily Mirror | 27p |
| First class post | 24p |
| Licence fee | 22p |

Source: BBC Facts and Figures 1992.

broadcasting services provided by the BBC. It is, for instance, substantially less than the average 40p a day minimum cost of subscribing to cable television, or the 92p a day which it costs to rent a satellite television dish and subscribe to the two movie channels. And if the licence fee maintains its current value in real terms, it will continue to decline as a proportion of broadcasting industry revenues throughout the 1990s. It could be as low as 25-30 per cent by the end of the decade.

## MIXED FUNDING?

While we believe that the licence fee is the best available mechanism for funding the BBC's core services, the BBC will also continue to pursue mixed funding. In our view, the licence fee should form part – albeit the major part – of a mixed funding base which should also contain supplementary funding for secondary distribution services with limited access.

The BBC already supplements the licence fee with other sources of income, primarily for services which are not universally accessible. This additional revenue is used not only to fund the secondary services in question, but also as a supplementary investment in programme making for the BBC's core services. As a consequence, the licence fee payer benefits both through a lower licence fee and a higher quality of programme making.

The BBC will therefore continue energetically to explore additional revenue streams. These will include:

- The reinvestment in domestic television and radio programmes of profits and cashflow from BBC Enterprises' successful programme sales, co-production and publishing businesses.

- An increasing stream of profits and programme investments from the BBC's participation in subscription television.

- Contractual payments from bilateral partners for the BBC's World Service Television outlets in several regions of the world.

- Gaelic Fund contributions for Gaelic language programming.

- Sponsorship of public arts and sporting events.

• • •

Viewed individually, each of the supplementary income streams is likely to appear modest relative to the BBC's overall funding needs. We have certainly found no evidence that they are likely to grow, either individually or collectively, to the point at which they would invalidate the need for the licence fee. However, taken together they can be an important supplement to the licence fee and form part of a genuinely mixed funding base for the full range of the BBC's services.

**The BBC will continue energetically to explore additional revenue streams**

# Direct Accountability

8

— **strong regulation**

— **clear performance objectives**

— **open communication**

In the 1990s all publicly funded organisations will be held directly accountable for the highest standards of performance against predefined objectives

This document sets out the purpose and objectives of the BBC as a publicly funded broadcaster. It provides the basis for what we believe should be the contract between the BBC and the licence payer over the next Charter period. The Charter Review process has clarified the need for this contract to be underpinned by a modern and effective system of accountability to the licence payer and to Parliament.

Such a system should take account of all the changes in the broadcasting environment described earlier, including the expansion of commercial broadcasting and the evolution of its regulatory regime. However, it should also take account of the particular responsibilities and requirements that are occasioned by public funding, and reflect the fact that in the 1990s all publicly funded organisations will be held directly accountable for the highest standards of performance against predefined objectives.

Accordingly, in this chapter we propose a number of changes that will strengthen the accountability of the BBC. They will do so in a way that reinforces its unique role and public purpose. In particular, we propose:

- A clarification of the separate roles played by the Board of Governors (acting as trustees of the public interest and as regulators) and the Board of Management (charged with the executive task of meeting an agreed set of performance objectives).

- A well defined framework of performance objectives and associated performance indicators against which BBC management can be held accountable.

- A new reporting structure encompassing appropriate mechanisms for communicating the BBC's objectives, and its performance against objectives, to the licence fee paying public.

This chapter elaborates each of these propositions and sets out new initiatives that the BBC intends to take.

SEPARATE ROLES FOR THE GOVERNORS AND MANAGEMENT

In earlier chapters of this document, we have proposed new objectives by which the BBC's performance should be judged. In the modern public service environment, it is clearly appropriate that the BBC's performance against those objectives should be accountable to a regulatory body, responsible directly to the licence payer and to Parliament. Such a regulatory body should hold the BBC's management to account, ensuring that it consistently meets its Charter obligations with programmes and services of the highest standard.

The BBC's Board of Governors has historically played this role, acting as the guardian of the public interest in the BBC's broadcasting activities – including the provision of redress for legitimate complaints. At the same time, it has also served to protect the independence of the BBC from government, political or commercial interference.

With the expansion of commercial broadcasting on both television and radio, a number of other bodies have been created to perform a regulatory function for commercial broadcasters and to safeguard minimum standards of public decency – for example, the ITC, the Radio Authority, the Broadcasting Standards Council (BSC) and the Broadcasting Complaints Commission (BCC).

There has been some suggestion that one or more of these bodies might have its powers extended to displace some or all of the traditional functions of the BBC Governors. For example:

■ **Some have suggested a single regulator for the whole broadcasting industry, which might regulate both publicly funded and commercially funded broadcasting, and which might take responsibility for setting the BBC's standards and for monitoring its performance.**

■ **Others have suggested a Public Service Broadcasting Authority, which would fund public service programmes made both by the BBC and by commercial broadcasters – effectively acting as a central allocator of licence fee and other public revenue.**

Both of these proposals have some potential advantages in clarifying the separation of roles between guardians of the public interest in broadcasting and the providers of broadcasting services. However, they also have a number of potential disadvantages. In particular:

■ **A single regulator for the whole industry would face the problem of taking two entirely different approaches to regulating commercial broadcasters and the BBC. For commercial broadcasters, it would have to define minimum standards. For the BBC, it would have to ensure an absolute commitment to the positive objectives of public service broadcasting.**

■ **Even when the BBC is pursuing its objective of extending choice and raising standards in broadcasting, its services will be competing for audiences with those of commercial broadcasters. A single regulator could face a conflict of interest between the need to ensure the success of commercial broadcasters and the obligation to support competitive services on the BBC.**

■ **The regulation of television and radio in the commercial sector is now the responsibility of separate bodies. Proposals for a single regulator for the whole of broadcasting would need to resolve whether BBC radio and BBC television should be regulated by one body or two, and which of these bodies, if any, should regulate World Service Radio and Television. The end result could be three different systems of regulation leading to potential confusion, additional bureaucracy and the possibility of diminishing the stature of the World Service, which is derived in great measure from its integration with the BBC's domestic services.**

■ **At present, the independence of the BBC from political or commercial interference is protected by its Charter and Board of Governors. A single regulator, with additional responsibilities for the commercial sector, could weaken this protection. It would also concentrate monopolistic regulatory power in one group. Without the stimulus of an** alternative regulatory regime it might become moribund, lacking the initiative and innovation that can be derived from different approaches.

■ Finally, any outside body – such as a Public Service Broadcasting Authority – which took on the additional role of allocating funds to programming proposals from other broadcasters alongside proposals from the BBC would require considerable organisational resources of its own. These would be likely to duplicate key functions of the BBC. It would need effectively to take on the roles of commissioning and scheduling programmes, for which the BBC is already equipped and skilled.

**The Governors have to act as trustees for the public interest**

While it is not for the BBC to define the regulatory framework in which it operates, we have drawn a number of lessons from this debate. In particular, if the BBC is to maintain the advantages that derive from an independent structure of regulation, it must clearly demonstrate that the BBC Governors are providing a regulatory challenge as tough as any independent regulator would provide. The Governors have to act as trustees for the public interest. They must hold the BBC accountable against the purpose and objectives defined in its Charter. This dictates the need to refine the respective roles of Governors and management – and the relationship between them.

In summary, we believe that the Board of Governors must be – and be seen to be – a body competent to assure the independence, integrity and performance standards of the BBC as a public corporation seeking to identify and meet the programme needs of viewers and listeners. Its primary responsibilities should be to ensure that the BBC's Charter obligations are appropriately translated into an overall mission and hierarchy of priorities; to review and approve the BBC's strategy on range, quality and funding of services; to set and monitor performance objectives on both programming standards and cost effectiveness; to report to licence payers and Parliament on performance against a clear set of external performance indicators; and to ensure that the BBC has the proper management in place. In addition, the Governors should continue to protect the BBC from external pressures, while providing final redress on complaints and compliance issues.

The Board of Management must collectively and individually perform the principal executive functions of the BBC, providing leadership and direction to the whole corporation. Its primary responsibilities should be to translate the BBC's mission and priorities into an overall strategy; to ensure the development and achievement of individual directorate plans for service and programme development; to run the services and operations to the highest standards of efficiency and productivity; and to report to the Board of Governors on all aspects of programming standards and cost effectiveness.

CREATING A CLEAR FRAMEWORK OF ACCOUNTABILITY

Such a clarification of the separate roles of Governors and management reveals the pivotal importance of a clear and coherent framework of accountability – a framework which the Governors can oversee and to which the management should be held accountable.

There is an increasing awareness of the need for public bodies such as the BBC to account for themselves directly to the public which provides their funding. That need for direct accountability applies equally to the quality and effectiveness of services and to the efficiency with which they are delivered.

In order for the BBC to meet its obligations of accountability, it must have a well-defined framework of objectives and performance indicators against which management can be held accountable. It is perhaps best to think of this framework as a pyramid of accountability.

At the apex of this pyramid should be those top line performance indicators on which the BBC as a whole should be held externally accountable – both to the licence payer and to Parliament. These indicators should relate directly to the strategic objectives that the BBC needs to pursue in order to meet its Charter obligations. The Board of Governors should report on these indicators of performance at the end of each year.

Further down this pyramid should be the more detailed objectives and measures against which individual BBC directorates and programme areas should be held internally accountable. These measures should cascade throughout the BBC organisation, and should reflect what each part of the BBC is expected to achieve.

For what, then, should the BBC be held accountable? It is clear that the BBC's Charter obligations to the licence payer and Parliament cannot be fulfilled simply by meeting the kind of audience share or ratings target which tends to predominate in the commercial broadcasting industry. As a publicly funded body, the BBC needs to meet a broader set of performance objectives that reflect its Charter obligations and priorities. We propose four sets of performance objectives against which the BBC should seek to meet agreed targets of achievement.

■ **Programming quality.** Is the BBC meeting its objectives of offering distinctive and high quality programmes in key areas? In particular:

— **Is the BBC providing an authoritative and trustworthy source of information?**

— **Is the BBC offering a valuable and enriching source of educational programming?**

— **Does the BBC provide access to the best of both classical and contemporary culture and entertainment?**

— **Does the BBC's scheduling of programmes, particularly in prime time, reflect its programming priorities?**

**The BBC must have a well-defined framework of objectives and performance indicators against which management can be held accountable**

■ **Audience value.** Is the BBC delivering value for money to the whole community? In particular:

— Does the BBC reach the whole community with something that they value?

— Does a significant proportion of the population regularly watch or listen to BBC services?

— Does the BBC have a significant and well-spread share of the national audience?

— Does the BBC adequately serve and reflect the nations and regions of the U.K. in its programming and resource allocation?

— Does the BBC reflect and serve appropriately a wide range of people with special needs and interests?

■ **Efficiency/effectiveness.** Is the BBC an efficient and cost effective organisation? In particular:

— Is the BBC efficient in the level and management of its overheads?

— Is the BBC productive in its programme making costs?

— Is the BBC cost effective in its transmission arrangements?

— Is the BBC capturing all of the available and appropriate opportunities to supplement the licence fee with commercial funding, within its overall funding policy?

— Does the BBC handle calls, correspondence and complaints from the public efficiently and effectively?

— Does the BBC represent best practice in its internal personnel and employment standards?

— Does the BBC manage its finances appropriately?

■ **International impact.** Is the BBC sustaining and developing its authority as an international source of information, culture and entertainment? In particular:

— Is the BBC World Service the most trusted among international broadcasters?

— Does the BBC World Service offer the broadest and most reliable news coverage among international broadcasters?

— Does the BBC World Service have the largest share of audience of international broadcasters?

— Does the BBC fully exploit the worldwide value of its programmes and services through appropriate commercial activities?

Information on the BBC's performance against these objectives should be collected regularly and consistently over time. That information should be used as the basis both of external reporting and of internal management scrutiny.

External reports by the BBC Governors should include both a qualitative assessment of the BBC's performance on each of these dimensions and the consistent reporting of reliable quantitative indicators of performance.

Internal reporting and management scrutiny should be facilitated by breaking down each 'top line' performance measure into successive levels of objectives and performance indicators within each BBC directorate, so that both Governors and managers can identify the source of any positive or adverse trend.

## REPORTING TO THE PUBLIC

Although the BBC is formally accountable to Parliament, it is ultimately accountable directly to the licence fee paying public that it serves. For that reason, it is important that the BBC should take the initiative to set out exactly what the public should expect from it and to report its performance against those objectives in an accessible way.

The BBC already employs a wide range of mechanisms to communicate with the public – its broadcast annual report programme 'See For Yourself'; television programmes like 'Biteback' and radio programmes like 'Feedback' which reflect the perspectives, and particularly the complaints, of viewers and listeners; the BBC's network of more than 60 advisory bodies – including local and regional groups and the Broadcasting Councils in Scotland, Wales and Northern Ireland – with membership drawn from all sections of the public; and the General Advisory Council, which is able to address the Governors and management of the BBC directly on matters of programme standards and policy.

Nevertheless, there is more that the BBC can and should do to report to the public. We propose the following initiatives:

- **A framework document on the BBC's governance and accountability. The BBC should publish a document that sets out the constitutional footing of the Corporation, and explains the separate roles and functions of the Governors and management. This document should also summarise the aims and objectives of the BBC and describe the arrangements for performance monitoring and reporting.**

- **A new system of complaint and redress, which should clarify how to make a complaint, explain how the BBC will respond to complaints and specify how it will make redress for serious mistakes. This system should ensure that viewers and listeners can complain directly to the relevant programme with the requirement for an early response; that they can receive an on-air correction where appropriate; and that they can 'appeal' to the Governors without prejudicing any complaint that they may wish to make to an outside body such as the Broadcasting Standards Council.**

- **A new, modernised system for licence fee payment, which should offer an easy payment scheme with the facility for monthly as well as quarterly payments by direct debit, as required.**

**The BBC is ultimately accountable directly to the licence fee paying public that it serves**

■  A transparent system of access to the BBC, which should be explained in terms of how to contact the BBC by telephone or letter, the maximum time allowed for a reply, and the guarantee of a courteous and personal response.

■  Annual reports on performance.  As described earlier the BBC should report regularly to the public on how it is performing against predefined targets on the provision of quality programming, audience value, efficiency and international impact.  These reports should be included in the annual report to licence payers and to Parliament, which – in addition to the BBC's financial accounts and a description of the BBC's activities during the year – should deliver a full assessment in qualitative and quantitative terms of performance against objectives.

●●●

This chapter has proposed an enhanced and modernised framework of governance and accountability for the BBC of the 1990s and beyond – a framework which reflects the BBC's unique status as a publicly funded broadcaster, and a contemporary approach to public service accountability.  We believe that it should serve to justify the public's continued confidence in, and funding of, the BBC.

# The Way Forward

This document has been about adaptation and change. It has described how the BBC needs to adapt its public purpose, its roles and objectives to reflect a new broadcasting environment; and how it needs to change its programmes and services to ensure that they achieve the BBC's primary aim of extending choice.

In the course of this document, we have outlined our initial views on each of the key questions about the future of the BBC. In summary, we have proposed that:

- **A publicly funded BBC should have a clear public purpose – namely to extend choice for viewers and listeners by guaranteeing universal access to programmes and services that would be at risk in a purely commercial market.**

- **In order to fulfil its public purpose, the BBC should focus its skills and resources on making and broadcasting high quality programmes that inform the national debate, express British culture and entertainment, create opportunities for education, and stimulate communication between the U.K. and abroad.**

- **The BBC should be a single, coherent broadcasting organisation, offering broadcasting services that are distinctive and focused on ensuring the range and volume of high quality programmes in each area.**

- **The BBC should meet the highest achievable standards of efficiency and cost effectiveness – and thus deliver outstanding value for money.**

- **The BBC should harness broadcasting technology to ensure that viewers and listeners receive the highest quality and most cost effective programmes and services.**

- **The BBC's core services should continue to be funded by the licence fee, but the licence fee should be supplemented by other sources of revenue – notably subscription fees – for secondary distribution services.**

- **Finally, the BBC's accountability to the licence payer and Parliament should be strengthened by the establishment of a detailed set of performance objectives, monitored by an independent Board of Governors, acting as trustees of the public interest and as regulators.**

These propositions represent our first contribution to the public discussion about the BBC's future role and services after 1996. We look forward to that discussion with enthusiasm. We expect to participate in it vigorously.

We have sought here to address the principal issues on which public discussion is likely to focus. What should be the BBC's public purpose? How should the BBC adapt its programmes and services in pursuit of this public purpose? How should the BBC develop its overseas role? How should it apply emerging technology to the task? How should it change the way it works to deliver superior value for money? How should the BBC be funded and at what level? And how should the BBC be held accountable to the licence payer and to Parliament?

## The Way Forward

The answers to these questions will go a long way to determining the shape of British broadcasting into the next century. The opportunity exists to define a clear and distinctive role for the BBC in the 1990s and beyond – and in doing so, to extend choice in broadcasting for everybody in the U.K.

**We would like to hear your views about the proposals in this document. Please write to: BBC, P.O. Box 1212, London W12 6AU.**

# Summary of Proposals

# Summary of Proposals

# Summary of Proposals

Over the years, the BBC has made a major contribution to British life. It is seen by many people as the world's leading broadcasting organisation. But British broadcasting is going through enormous changes and, at the same time, the BBC's Charter is due to be renewed at the end of 1996. Against this background, the BBC has carried out a thorough review of its role and services.

## THE CHANGING CONTEXT

- By the year 2000, most households will be able to receive 20 television channels and 15 radio stations.

- Some television stations will offer general entertainment for large audiences, but an increasing number will be specialist channels for different interest groups.

- Most radio stations will offer different types of pop and popular music.

- There will be much stronger competition for commercial revenue to support these channels and stations.

- Experience from other countries which have been through similar changes suggests that, whilst more services can lead to greater choice, increased competition can also lead to less investment in programmes of quality for the domestic market.

- As the society it serves develops and as the broadcasting market expands, the BBC must adapt – as it has done in the past – to these different circumstances.

## A CLEAR PUBLIC PURPOSE FOR THE BBC

- Within their contractual obligations to regulators, and their own concern for the public interest, commercially funded broadcasters quite properly give highest priority to producing and scheduling programmes in order to make a profit.

- In contrast, publicly funded broadcasters have an obligation only to the public.

- Both types of broadcaster have complementary roles to play, but the balance between them will change as the commercial sector expands.

- The expansion of commercial broadcasting will not invalidate the need for publicly funded broadcasting, but it will serve more clearly to limit and define its role.

- In the past, with limited competition, the BBC had a duty to cover all audiences and broadcasting needs.

- In the future, there is a clear public purpose for the BBC. It should extend choice for viewers and listeners by guaranteeing access for everyone in the country to programme services that are of unusually high quality and that are, or might be, at risk in a purely commercial market.

■ The BBC will therefore focus its activities on four key roles, aiming to set standards in each of these major programme areas. It will offer:

■ A wide range of news, current affairs and information programming, which includes:

— **Journalism of impartiality and authority.**

— **Programming which reports, analyses and debates the main issues of the day.**

— **The investigation of social, economic and cultural issues.**

— **Regional and local journalism.**

■ Fresh and innovative entertainment and a showcase for both traditional and contemporary British culture, including:

— **A wide range of drama on television and radio.**

— **Pioneering comedy and light entertainment.**

— **Performance and coverage of music and the arts.**

— **Authoritative and creative coverage of sport.**

— **A unique service for children and young people.**

■ Specialist and general programmes that help to educate their audience, including:

— **Science and natural history.**

— **Social and political history.**

— **Religious, moral and ethical programming.**

— **Documentaries and features.**

— **Schools and Open University programmes.**

— **Programmes which enhance the nation's vocational skill base.**

■ Programmes and services which communicate between the U.K. and the rest of the world, including:

— **World Service Radio, which is the world's most trusted and listened to international source of information, culture and entertainment.**

— **The continuing development of World Service Television.**

— **Increasing involvement in the international market for programme sales and co-productions.**

— **Programmes which reflect the rest of the world to British audiences.**

■ The BBC should evolve and adapt its services to deliver these priorities and objectives. Over time, it should withdraw from programme areas or types in which it is no longer able or needed to make an original contribution.

■ The BBC cannot fulfil its role, though, if it is forced only to provide programmes for a cultural elite. It must maintain regular contact with all viewers and listeners, providing value through its services to as many people as possible. But it should do so in a way which places the greatest importance on developing services of distinction and quality, rather than on attracting a large audience for its own sake.

## A SINGLE COHERENT BROADCASTING ORGANISATION

■ A single BBC brings the following benefits:

— **A single, coherent role and strategy for publicly funded broadcasting in the U.K.**

— **Concentrated investment in specialist skills and expertise at a level which could not be duplicated by a number of smaller organisations.**

— **The extended use of that specialist expertise across all of the BBC's radio and television channels to deliver the best possible programming to each audience.**

— **Complementary scheduling of programmes across radio and television to ensure maximum choice for viewers and listeners, particularly at peak times.**

— **A coherent range of radio, television and other programme services for people overseas.**

## THE BBC'S SERVICES

■ The BBC's services must be scheduled and organised in a complementary manner. But they must also have individual identities and priorities:

**BBC 1** – should be the BBC's main national television channel delivering distinctive, quality programming to a wide audience.

**BBC 2** – should be the more innovative, experimental channel addressing different groups within the audience.

■ On network radio the BBC should adapt and change its services as the marketplace around it changes. In doing so, it should give priority to services which are unlikely ever to be matched in the commercial marketplace. These services should include:

— **A quality speech network which carries news and current affairs, magazine programmes, documentaries, drama, comedy, entertainment and special interest programmes.**

- A network which broadcasts a wide range of high quality live and recorded classical music and cultural programming.

- A continuous news network.

- Distinctive and innovative services which include:

  • Pop and popular music programming of range, diversity and innovation.

  • Specialist music programming.

  • An emphasis on live performance, new work and ideas.

  • A higher degree of speech content than commercial music stations, including news and information, humour, drama and social action.

  • Clearly informative and intelligent presentation.

- Educational programmes.

- Sports coverage.

- A major commitment to British culture and the arts, including support for the role of the BBC Orchestras in the national pattern of orchestral funding and provision.

■ In regional broadcasting the BBC should:

- Commission and make network programmes right across the country to ensure that it reflects to a national audience the regional and cultural diversity which enriches the U.K.

- Deliver an increasingly high quality daily regional television news service, together with weekly current affairs and Parliamentary programmes.

- Complete the move of its local radio stations to 100 per cent speech at key times, offering:

  • High quality journalism.

  • A focal point for community debate and action.

  • A voice for the country's multi racial and multi lingual groups.

- Invest in high quality information, cultural and entertainment programming for Scotland, Wales and Northern Ireland.

■ The BBC should play an increasingly active role in secondary distribution markets as an important dimension of its public service purpose and in order to generate additional funds for reinvestment in new programming. In particular, it should:

- Continue to develop its successful participation in the markets for programme related publications and products within a clear commercial framework.

— Take part in the development of commercially funded specialist television services on satellite and cable. Examples include:

- A continuous news service.

- Channels which draw on the BBC's archives – like the collaboration with Thames Television to launch U.K. Gold.

■ In its overseas operations, the BBC should:

— Support, extend and enhance World Service Radio.

— Develop World Service Television.

— Intensify the BBC's participation in the international market for programme sales and co-productions.

## HARNESSING TECHNOLOGY

■ At least three major new technological initiatives are under way:

— High definition/widescreen television which can offer enhanced quality pictures.

— Digital television which could dramatically increase the number of services available to viewers.

— Digital audio broadcasting which could dramatically increase the number, quality and convenience of radio services.

■ It is not clear how quickly these improvements will become available to the mass market.

■ The BBC's future approach to technology should continue to be driven by the objective of providing high quality, cost effective programmes and services to viewers and listeners.

## THE BBC'S FUNDING

■ The BBC has examined a number of options for its future funding. The review has concluded that:

— Commercial funding methods such as subscription, sponsorship and advertising affect the types of programmes which are made and broadcast.

— There will not be sufficient advertising or similar forms of revenue to sustain the wide range of television and radio services that the public will wish to enjoy in the future.

— Therefore, the licence fee remains the best available mechanism for preserving the BBC's independence from political or commercial pressure, guaranteeing universal access and maintaining a wide range of broadcasting in the U.K.